ROSES IN DECEMBER

ROSES IN DECEMBER

Prose and Verse
Clarine Coffin Grenfell

Clarine Coffin Grenfell

wishing you beautiful 'Roses'

when your 'December' comes

for Adrienne

beautiful Christian woman

Roses:
Lornagrace Grenfell Bowron

Snowflakes:
Lunette Fifield, Helga Johnson

Additional titles by the same author:
The Caress and the Hurt
Women My Husband Married

A Publication Of
GRENFELL READING CENTER
Alamoosook Lake
Orland, Maine 04472

LIBRARY OF CONGRESS CATALOG NUMBER: 83-904-561
ISBN NUMBER: 0-9612766-1-4
PRINTED IN THE UNITED STATES OF AMERICA BY
LITHOGRAPHICS, INC., CANTON, CT 06019

. . . for all lonely ones

who hold in their heart with remembered joy

yet sometimes water with silent tears

their roses in December

CONTENTS

ROSES IN DECEMBER

The days are closing in, pale narrow days—
Late dawn, a few brief hours, then early dusk . . . .

Here in our northern town the flower shops
Are riotous with color—orange, pink,
Deep purple, lavender, red, yellow, blue—
Last summer's bloom impaled on thin steel wires.
I do not need a dried bouquet, dead flowers.

Pulsing and warm against all darkness, cold,
Vibrant and bright against all sunless hours,
Are memories of those I've loved . . . and so
For living roses here in my December,
I've only to think of you . . . only to remember . . . .

Alamoosook Lake
Orland, Maine
December, 1983

"Fame is the scentless sunflower,
with gaudy crown of gold;
But friendship is the breathing rose,
with sweets in every fold."
Oliver Wendell Holmes

'NOT AN ATTORNEY—A PUBLISHER!'

Marjorie Mueller Freer often scolds me. Closest and best friend for some thirty years, she has, of course, earned the right. Of German descent, her own life always planned far in advance, always meticulously organized, she most often scolds me for my haphazard ways.

Marjorie is a devotee of yard sales. That day I'd driven her to three and in between each one I'd been badgered because I've never made a will.

"Don't you care," she asked, "what becomes of your goods, your treasures?"

"What treasures? Like those?" I gestured toward the back seat, piled high with lamps that would probably never again light, cameras that would probably never again click, picnic baskets without handles.

"Of course not. Things you value. Your antiques—your treasures!"

"I've got an antique foot tub I treasure very much. It belonged to my great-great-great-aunt, and when I get home, I'm going to fill it with hot water and soak my antique feet in it. Your yard sales are wearing me out, Marj."

"Joke if you like, but you know I'm right. Look around . . . you'll see what I mean. . . ."

So when I got home, I filled Aunt Fanny's foot tub with hot water, sat down and looked around. Treasures . . . things I value . . . did I really have anything worth calling an attorney for, worth putting into a will?

This tub, I thought, blissfully moving my toes up and down . . . *and this lamp.* The day was waning. I reached up, turned the switch. A soft glow fell on a small, pearl-handled knife, an ivory box, red and yellow roses on its cover . . . *Dad's pen-knife and shaving kit—I treasure those. Can still see him peeling apples, still smell his shaving cream . . . memories,* I thought, *memories and roses. . . . What was it Sir James Barrie had said? . . .* **"God gave us memory that we might have roses in December. . . ."**

I looked around the room again. Was there really anything of value? . . . two cranberry-glass vases filled with ivy, a bit of drift-wood, the Log Book from Alamoo, Tom Kurti's poems, a thick let-ter from Pamela in faraway California, a red clay pot that had once held tulips, an old silver tray, *"With our utmost devotion, the Class of 1955"* . . . treasures to me, of course, things I value . . . but for their memories, not themselves . . . an attorney would surely laugh. . . . My things were simply 'roses in December.' I reached for a pen, a pad of yellow paper, began writing. . . .

Marjorie called the next morning. "Have you looked around?" she asked in her scolding voice. "Thought any more about making a will? Thought about your treasures?"

"Yes, Marj—I've been thinking quite a bit about them."

"Well, are you going to call an attorney? Put them in a will?"

"No, dear. I'm going to call a publisher—put them in a book."

"A book?"

"Yes, I hope you'll like the title. I'm going to call it **Roses in De-cember.** . . ."

LEARNING TO LIVE

THE TRUE, THE DIFFERENT VIEW

For Georgia O'Keeffe

I see you walking city streets at night
On Stieglitz' arm, face tilted toward the light
Of distant stars, a full white moon that you
Will keep from ever waning, ever new . . . .

In Taos now you gaze into far space . . .
Badlands, wastelands, a desolate barren place
You'll paint in blue, red, yellow, purple, green—
Bright colors none but you had ever seen . . . .

Now you hold a shell, a wild flower in your hands—
Now pry a long-dead skull from desert sands—
Finding in each life's lovely symmetry
Unseen until you paint and make us see.

Our universe is changed because of you
Who give blind eyes the true, the different view.

WE GIVE THEM THINGS

We give them things when they go away. Not for them—
"Take this," we say, "or this, or this, oh, please—
Would you like this plain glass lamp? this silver tray?
There's a story, of course—do you have time to hear?"

We give them things when they go away. Not for them—
"Look around," we say. "Is there something here you'd like?
This old foot tub? this braided rug? It's worn . . .
This vase? this ivory fan? A clipper ship
Once carried it halfway around the world . . .
There's a story, of course, do you have time to hear?"

We give them things when they go away—not for them,
But for ourselves! "Take this!" we say. "Oh, please—
Into your distant life far down the years
Take some small part of mine! Remember me!
Give it some day to some child yet unborn.
Give it and say, 'She gave me this one day
As I was going away.' Say, 'There's a story, of course . . .
Do you have time—do you have time to hear?'"

"Now the bright morning star, Day's harbinger,
Comes dancing from the East, and leads with her
The flowery May, who from her green lap throws
The yellow cowslip and the pale primrose."

John Milton

THE PLAIN GLASS LAMP

We did not have electricity at 782 Broadway until 1920. For the first ten years of my life, the plain glass lamp stood at the top of the curved stairwell leading from downstairs where our parents slept, to upstairs where we children slept. "Be careful of the lamp," my mother often said. "It's there in case you're ever sick in the night and need us." I needed my parents one night when I was four. I was not sick, but I needed them, especially my mother.

She had gone downtown that afternoon, left Merle, five years older, in charge. Like Mama, I loved pretty dishes, especially those behind the glass doors of her square oak china closet in the dining room. Of course, I was forbidden to open those doors, to touch those precious dishes, but at some unguarded point during the long afternoon I had disobeyed—opened the glass doors, lifted up the fragile, four-sided cream pitcher, admired the dainty pink roses painted on each side. It was my favorite dish.

Of course, I dropped it. It lay there on the carpet before my frightened eyes in two pieces, the handle quite knocked off. What to do . . . . Mama could spank very hard when she was angry, and this was one of her favorite dishes, too.

What I had done was pick up both pieces, put the handle inside, put the pitcher back on the shelf, handleless side turned carefully toward the back.

That night Mama heard our *'Now I lay me down to sleep,'* tucked my sister Jill and me into bed, went downstairs. Jill fell asleep in minutes, but I could not. For what seemed hours I lay listening to the murmur of my parents' voices, coming up from the kitchen through the round register in our bedroom floor.

Jill and I sometimes lay on our bellies, ears over the register, listening to those voices. One night not long before, the dust had sent Jill into a coughing spell. My father had called in a stern voice, "Go to bed up there! Don't let me hear a pin drop!" Jill had gone dutifully to bed, but I had found the pincushion on my bureau, pulled out a common pin, pushed it through the grating, let go.

The **Prodigal Son** lamp always stood at the head of the stairs. "Take it," Mother said, "and the shaving kit, too. You always liked roses."

The pearl-handled knife, the bowl of apples, Papa's oak Morris chair with the gargoyle arms.

14

"Did you hear it drop?" I'd called saucily down as the pin bounced on the black stovetop beneath.

My father had come upstairs then, sat beside my bed, explained the word *eavesdropping*. "Listening to other people talk when they don't know you're there," he'd said, "is a sneaky thing to do."

Turning pitchers so their broken handles don't show is a sneaky thing, too, I was sure. Time and again I closed my eyes, tried to sleep . . . could not . . . 'In case you ever need us in the night—' my mother had said.

Well, it was night—and I needed her, needed to be forgiven. I slipped out of bed at last, crept around the lamp, down the dim stairwell, one hand grasping the banister . . . through the hall, through the dining room with its guilty secret, flung open the kitchen door.

"Why, Clarine, what's the matter?"

"Are you sick, dear?"—my mother's hand quick on my forehead.

"Mama—Mama—I broke the pitcher!"

Over the years I have taught the story of the Prodigal Son many times to Sunday School classes. When I teach it, I don't see a young man going off to the city, coming back in rags and tatters. Rather I see a fearful child in a small white nightgown, creeping around a kerosene lamp, down a dim stairwell . . . throwing open a door to light, to warmth, to embracing arms, to forgiveness.

I had not 'wasted my substance on wine and women,' had not 'eaten with the swine.' But I had sinned and been repentant, confessed and been forgiven.

The plain glass lamp is 'electrified' now and sits here on my table. A Bible is nearby. Sometimes I read again by its light the most moving story ever told—the story of a father's forgiveness:

"Bring forth the best robe, and put it on him; and put a ring on his finger, and shoes on his feet:

And bring hither the fatted calf, and kill it; and let us eat and be merry:

For this my son was dead, and is alive again; he was lost and is found. And they began to be merry."

Luke 15:22-24

I call it my 'Prodigal Son' lamp . . . and, remembering the sweetness of my mother's forgiveness, cherish it as one of my 'roses in December.'

"Gather ye rosebuds while ye may,
Old Time is still a-flying:
And this same flower that smiles today
Tomorrow will be dying."

Robert Herrick

THE PEARL-HANDLED KNIFE

"Mama, do you feel able to come for a little ride?" Ninety now, my mother seldom left her room, but she had just given me a new bright blue station wagon and I wanted her to ride in it. "Apple trees are all in bloom—" I added.

"Could we ride through the fields, up at the old place? Would it hurt the car?"

"Not a bit. Every rock was picked out of those fields a hundred years ago, and Lloydie keeps them mowed smooth as glass.

"He loves to ride around on his machines. . . ." So we drove from 656 Broadway, mother's new house, to 782 Broadway, 'the old place'—built in 1852 by Captain Daniel K. Pomroy's ship's carpenters for his bride, Margaret Gulliver, my great-grandmother. My mother and father had moved into it in 1906, three years after their own marriage. Mama had owned it for fifty years, all six of her children born in the front bedroom of that house. In the early fifties Lloyd, second son, and his wife Margaret had bought it from her, still lived there.

"Lloyd hasn't plowed up much of a garden."

"No, Mama—not like the acres Old Maude used to plow."

"Old Maude—haven't thought of her for years."

"I used to ride her all over these fields in Lloyd's ROTC uniform. Always had trouble winding the puttees. . ."

"Smell the blossoms!" Mama drew deep breaths as, all the windows of the new wagon rolled down, I drove slowly past the MacIntosh Reds, the Yellow Transparents, the Red Astrachans.

"Do you remember, Mama," I asked, pink and white blossoms falling on the bright blue paint, "how the apple peelings used to smell when Papa tossed them on the Clarion?"

"You each got a penny if the peeling broke—" Mama laughed . . . and suddenly the orchard is echoing with laughter and I am sitting in a high-backed oak chair in the kitchen at 782, my sister and brothers all gathered around Papa as he takes from his vest pocket a small pearl-handled knife, unclasps it. . . .

16

Millard F. Coffin

Clara B. Kelly

Married

Wednesday, September Thirtieth

nineteen hundred and three

Bangor, Maine

At Home, 195 Pine Street
October tenth

*"I'd put on Lloyd's ROTC uni-
form, ride Old Maude all over
these fields . . . always had trou-
ble with the puttees!"*

17

"Do we get pennies if the peeling breaks?" Millard, Jr., always the financier, wants to know.

"Of course!" Papa jingles the pennies in his pocket.

"Thomasin Sweets tonight, Papa." Merle comes clattering up from the cellar, the wooden bowl in his hands heaped high with apples. "They're just right."

"Thanks, son. Bart's apple first." The tiny blade moves round and round. Bart, long red curls bouncing, watches from Papa's knee as the thin yellow coil grows longer, longer. . . . "Think I'm going to make it tonight . . . easy now . . . almost, almost . . . Aw, shucks!"

The yellow peeling breaks, falls sizzling on the hot stovetop.

Bart shrieks with laughter, holds out his hand for his penny, runs to push it into his piggy bank. *Why*, we older ones sometimes wonder, *does Bart's peeling seem to break oftener than anyone else's? Is it because he's the youngest?*

But tonight Millard, Jr.'s peeling breaks, too. Delighted, he runs for his bank, pushes in the penny, shakes hard to see how full it is. Peeling after peeling falls on the stove. The smell of burning apple fills the room.

"Did you feel the Porters, son?"

"Hard as rocks, Papa. And so are the Blue Pearmains. But the Bellflowers are softening up."

"Mama'll want them for her Thanksgiving pies—won't you, Clara?"

"Anything but Wolf Rivers!" Mama, pumping water at the sink, answers. "You can feed those to the pigs as far as I'm concerned. Big and showy and not a bit of taste to 'em . . . Come, children. Time to brush your teeth, go to bed . . . Just be sure, Millie," she adds, "to save the Russets for Christmas. . . ."

"Where are the Russet trees?" I asked Mama now as we turned back toward Broadway.

"All dead. Lloyd had them cut down."

"I can still remember the taste of those little brown apples, Mama. We always had them at Christmas."

"Would you like your father's pearl-handled knife?" she asked, back in her bedroom.

"You know I would, Mama."

She lay back on the pillow, exhausted. "It's there on the bureau—in his old shaving kit, the one with the cabbage roses. May as well take that, too, dear. I remember you always liked roses. . . ."

"When I am dead, my dearest,
Sing no sad songs for me;
Plant thou no roses at my head,
Nor shady cypress tree . . . ."

Christina Rossetti

THE FOOT TUB

"He riseth from supper and laid aside his garments; and took a
towel and girdeth himself.
After that he poureth water into a basin, and began to wash the
disciples' feet, and to wipe them with the towel wherewith he was
girded."   John 13:4-5

My Aunt Fanny was reading me this story as I knelt on a braided rug in her kitchen, the white enamel foot tub before me. I rubbed the uneven cake of homemade soap hard on the wash rag to make suds. I did not like the smell of Aunt Fanny's feet when I first pulled off her white cotton stockings, but the glycerin and rose water my mother put into her soap soon covered up the smell of feet, just as it covered up the smell of the old bacon fat and lye Mama used to make soap.

Then, too, waves of clove, nutmeg, cinnamon, and one other delicious smell were coming from the oven where our venison mince pies baked. Aunt Fanny always had some treat baking in the oven while I washed her feet.

Today she had let me make my own small pie for Papa's Thanksgiving dinner. Papa gave Aunt Fanny the venison for her mincemeat, liked hers better than Mama's. Mama said that wasn't fair—Maine was a temperance state and Aunt Fanny had no business lacing her mincemeat with brandy. I liked Aunt Fanny's mincemeat better, too. Now, waiting for my treat to bake, I beat the soapsuds into a high lather. Washing her feet once a week was the treat I gave Aunt Fanny, for she was far too old and fat to bend down and bathe them herself. I was eight and could do it quite easily.

I can still see her feet—short, wide, and stubby, the toes almost even across the top, the skin like yellowed paper, the blue veins under it almost purple. I didn't mind washing Aunt Fanny's feet because she read to me while I was doing it, often the same story she was reading today. Sometimes she taught me some old song, singing the words in a high, cracked voice. I knew eight verses of

19

Over the River and through the Wood and planned to sing that song to my Papa that afternoon after dinner. The story was ending.
. . .

"So after he had washed their feet, and had taken his garments and was set down again, he said unto them, Know ye what I have done to you?

Ye call me Master and Lord: and ye say well, for so I am. If I then, your Master and Lord, have washed your feet, ye also ought to wash one another's feet.

Verily, verily, I say unto you, The servant is not greater than his lord; neither he that is sent greater than he that sent him.

If ye know these things, happy are ye if ye do them."

John 13:12-17

I did not know exactly what 'Verily, verily' meant, but I liked the sound of the words, and I always felt happy when I'd finished washing Aunt Fanny's feet. I was sure she loved me, that I was her special little girl. She often showed me the tin picture of her only daughter Nellie who had died when a child, and Walter, her son, had two boys, no girls.

Now—prying stubby toes apart with small fingers, sprinkling cornstarch from a yellow box between each one, pulling on the clean white cotton stockings—I felt happy, as the story said, for doing these things.

"Thank you, child. Empty the water and we'll see if the pies are browned." I carried the tub outside, wiped up the spots of soap-suds from the wide yellow boards of Aunt Fanny's kitchen floor, and joined her before the black oven door with *Clarion* printed on it.

"Just one letter different from your name," Aunt Fanny re-minded me again. "Ah—brown as a berry. Go choose your cup while I make the tea."

Aunt Fanny kept her five best cups on the pine chest in her din-ing room. Days I washed her feet I could drink from any one. "Bone China," she'd say, holding a cup up to the light. "Look, child! So thin you can see right through it!" Her father, Captain Benjamin Gulliver, Aunt Fanny said, had used these cups in his captain's quarters on the long voyage from Scotland to America more than a hundred years before.

The dining room was cold. I reached quickly for my favorite cup, the one with pink roses inside and out. Aunt Fanny filled it with tea, added milk. Now I could not see the inside roses until I'd drunk every drop. Then we carried our mince pies, hers big, mine small, down the street to my own house for Papa's Thanksgiving dinner.

Aunt Fanny spent the last of her more than ninety years in that house, lovingly cared for by my mother. When my wedding day came, she was in her Mount Hope grave, but foot tub and bread board were passed along to me. In the years since then, they have traveled with me to nine different homes. Now this year, 1979, three small Grenfell grandchildren are traveling from Maine to Connecticut to spend Thanksgiving with Grandpa and me.

We are excited about their coming, have made many preparations—stuffed a turkey, opened the last jar of my mother's venison mincemeat, well laced with the no longer illegal brandy. These granddaughters—Tamarleigh Grace, almost eight, and the six-year-old twins, Tallessyn Zawn and Trelawney Jean—all love to sing, know the words of many old songs. I'm almost sure that tomorrow, as we roll out piecrust on her bread board, they'll be singing to Grandpa and me eight verses of the same Thanksgiving song Aunt Fanny taught me when I, too, was eight years old. . . .

Aunt Fanny's house, the first house on Outer Broadway, built in the early 1800's by my great-great grandfather, Captain Benjamin Gulliver, Scotsman.

All: *Over the river and through the wood,*
To grandmother's house we go!
The horse knows the way
To carry the sleigh
Through the white and drifted snow.

T.G.: *Over the river and through the wood,*
To have a first-rate play.
Hear the bells ring,
"Ting-a-ling-ding!"
Hurrah for Thanksgiving Day!

T.J.: *Over the river and through the wood*
And straight through the barnyard gate.
We seem to go
Extremely slow—
It is so hard to wait!

T.Z.: *Over the river and through the wood,*
When grandmother sees us come,
She will say, "Oh, dear,
The children are here!
Bring a pie for everyone!"

All: *Over the river and through the wood,*
Now grandmother's cap I spy!
Hurrah for the fun!
Is the pudding done?
Hurrah for the pumpkin pie!

My feet will probably be a bit weary tomorrow from all the Thanksgiving preparations. Perhaps after dinner I will take down the white enamel foot tub, fill it with hot water, sit and tell three children about Carolyn Frances Gulliver Barker, their great-great-great-great-great Aunt Fanny . . . perhaps even read them the story she so often read to me . . . the story about a man who girded himself with a towel, knelt down before a basin . . . a man who said, *"If ye know these things, happy are ye if ye do them."*

MY ROCK

When I was nine, my grandmother took my hand,
Walked me beside the sea, gave me a rock—
"This is your rock," she said. "You must know it well.
A glacier carried it five thousand miles
From Hudson Bay, perhaps from the very Pole,
Then dropped it here for me to give to you.
Oh, yes, perhaps some Indian girl once climbed
Its granite sides, lay on it, called it hers,
And perhaps long years from now some other girl
May claim it for her own. But for your life,
Your little span of years, this rock is yours.
Now scramble up . . . ."

                    "Does it have a name?" I asked.
"A secret name—some call it Work, some Truth,
Some call it Love—but you'll not know its name
Till you are old and have built your life on it.
Now lie face down. Do you see the tiny specks,
Bright crystals shining in the sun? That's quartz.
You'll study rocks in school someday. Turn now
And face the sky. Spread wide your arms. Do you feel
The rock beneath you—hard, unyielding, firm?
Say: This is the rock my grandmother gave to me."
This is the rock my grandmother gave to me.
"Through every shifting sand that I must walk,"
Through every shifting sand that I must walk,
"This rock will hold me up. This is my rock."
This rock will hold me up. This is my rock.

*"Faith is like a lily lifted high and white,
Love is like a lovely rose, the world's delight."*
Christina Rossetti

"TOMORROW NIGHT IT'LL BE YOUR TURN"

By midnight Christmas Eve Summerfield Methodist Church on
Staten Island was packed. My son and I were sharing his popular
Candlelight Service, I behind the pulpit on the right, he behind the
lectern on the left. The Order of Worship was in my hands, but the
candlelight was too dim for me to read it.

"May the Lord bless to our understanding this reading of His
Holy Word." John finished the Christmas Scripture, turned slightly
toward the right, toward me. *Scripture—then Prayer*, I thought,
jumped to my feet, said in a loud voice—I dislike women ministers
who can't be heard!—"Let us be in the spirit of prayer!"

I prayed for some time. When I finished, my son turned again to
the right, lifted the brass offering plates from the altar table, beck-
oned the eight waiting ushers to come forward.

"My mother," he smiled at the congregation, "is always very
quick to pray. We will now receive the Christmas Eve offering."

The Christmas Eve offering! Much of the church budget might
depend on it! What had I done? I held the Order of Worship close
to a flickering candle. 'Quick to pray'—I certainly had been! So
quick I'd jumped over not only the offering but also the guest solo-
ist and the Doxology.

'Quick to pray'—it was not always so. My mind raced back over
the years. . . .

I am fourteen, sitting by an ornate parlor stove in the home of
Lunette Fifield, seventy and recently widowed. Mrs. Fifield has
been my piano teacher for two years. Famous for her tatted snow-
flakes, she had sometimes given me one when I'd practiced hard,
had a particularly good lesson. Now she is to be more than piano
teacher. That afternoon I've come to live with her during my junior
year at Bangor High School. . . .

As I did my homework after supper, Mrs. Fifield sat tatting
snowflakes, her ivory shuttle flashing in and out with the fine
white thread. When I finished, she laid aside her tatting, lifted two
warm flat soapstones from the top of the parlor stove, wrapped
them in scorched flannel.

"Run up and put one in each bed," she handed them to me.
"Then we'll have our evening devotions. I'll ask you to read a
chapter from *Luke*."

24

Evening devotions—this was something new. My evening devotions had ended when I was about four, about the time Mama, busy with three younger children, had left me to kneel down and say my own *'Now I lay me down to sleep. / I pray the Lord my soul to keep.'* I'd knelt till cold weather came, then as the linoleum on my Maine bedroom floor got chillier and chillier, I'd skipped the kneeling, hopped under the blankets for my rote prayer. After awhile, I'd skipped that, too.

But I loved to read aloud—I was supposed to be very good at 'elocution'—so I slipped the warm soapstones between the icy blankets and came happily back to the glowing coals in the parlor stove to read my chapter in *Luke*.

Mrs. Fifield folded her hands when I'd finished, closed her eyes and prayed—a fairly long prayer. *How*, I wondered, *can she think of so many things to pray about?* She thanked God for my brother Merle, who'd brought my things in the wagon, for the music and the meals we would share in the coming weeks. She asked God to help me do my homework, help me worship Him with 'all my mind.' She prayed I would not be homesick for my family—and on and on and on. At the end we said the *Lord's Prayer* together. Then she went to the piano, opened the hymnal.

"Play this one, Clarine—*Now the Day Is Over*. It's hard—three sharps, but it's a good one to go to bed by. . . ."

> *"Through the long night watches*
> *May Thine angels spread*
> *Their white wings above me,*
> *Watching round my bed.*
>
> *When the morning wakens,*
> *Then may I arise*
> *Pure and fresh and sinless*
> *In Thy holy eyes."*

I felt very good as we climbed the stairs together. Mrs. Fifield might be an old, old lady, but I was going to like living with her. Then she turned, said casually over her shoulder, "I'll read the Scripture tomorrow night, Clarine. It'll be your turn to say the prayer."

Suddenly I did not feel so good. My turn to say the prayer? A long, long prayer like hers?

"My turn?"

"Yes, dear. We'll alternate."

I undressed quickly, put my cold feet on the soapstones. I had

25

both kinds of cold feet—inside and out. Tomorrow night—my turn! What in the world would I say? Certainly not *"Now I lay me down to sleep!"* That was a baby prayer and I was fourteen years old. And not the *Lord's Prayer*—we'd said that one together. What then?

I tried to remember all the things Mrs. Fifield had prayed about. She'd gone right through the whole day! I went to sleep after awhile, my feet on the comforting warm flannel and in my heart the first spontaneous prayer I'd prayed in years: *Dear God, please help me to pray to You tomorrow."*

The next day I tried to keep a list in my head of things to pray about. School, of course. I liked all my teachers—Miss Webster, Latin, Miss DuBoshier, geometry, Madame Beaupre, French, Mrs. Carroll, English. Bangor High was on half-sessions all during my high-school years. When I came home that noon, Mrs. Fifield had made a steamed apple pudding. I could certainly thank God for that!

"You must be tired from school, dear," she said after lunch. "Lie down on the sitting-room couch and take a nap." She half closed the inside blinds, spread an afghan over me. This had certainly never happened to me before! *Must remember to thank God for it*, I thought drowsily, going off to sleep.

Piano music woke me an hour later. "We'll have a short lesson," Mrs. Fifield said, "then go to the library. You must keep better time, Clarine—keep the beat! It doesn't matter if you miss a note or two in the bass, but if you're going to play hymns in church, you must keep the beat!" She seemed very sure that I was someday going to play hymns in church.

At the library I lay on the rug by the fire in the Children's Room while Mrs. Fifield picked out books. "A new Grace Richmond," she said with satisfaction on the way home, "and they say Gene Stratton-Porter is publishing a new one, too." *Writers*, I thought—*Must remember to thank God for them.*

We stopped for a few minutes at Miss Amanda Wilson's house. She gave us tea and cookies and, as we were leaving, pushed a folded wad of paper into my hand. "So glad dear Lunette is not going to be alone," she whispered to me.

On the street I unfolded the paper. A dollar bill! Mrs. Fifield was as delighted as I. The list in my head was growing longer and longer. If I could remember everything that night, I guessed I'd be able to pray long enough. . . .

During the time I lived with Mrs. Fifield, I was cared for, taught, loved, but never exploited. Coal fires burned in kitchen and parlor stoves. Heavy hods of coal must have been carried daily up the steep cellar stairs. I never saw this being done, was never asked to do it. Heedless, I never thought to offer.

I was asked to do a few things—kneel down on winter nights and fasten 'grippers' around the soles of black-buckled galoshes so we could walk along to Wednesday night prayer meetings at the Pine Street Methodist Church. I did not pray aloud there that first year, though. Mr. Clinton Baldwin, the leader—tall, white-haired, stern—terrified me. I could pray with God and Mrs. Fifield listening, but not with God and Mr. Baldwin.

June 15, 1926, I showed my father my report card for the year. He examined it for several minutes.

"Nothing but *A*'s, eh. Well, that's not so bad, is it, dear." He handed the card back to me. Maine people never gush. I knew I had been highly praised.

I remember that date and my father's words that night because they were the last he ever said to me. He died just before midnight—a sudden, unexpected heart attack. I was glad that night that I could talk to God in other words than '*Now I lay me—*'

During my senior year with Mrs. Fifield I finally found courage to talk to Him in front of Mr. Baldwin. Nine years later in 1935 I resigned my teaching job at Bangor High School—"No one," my mother said tartly, "*resigns* a job!"—went to theological seminary . . . became a pastor of churches . . . offered many public prayers . . . met and married a pastor of churches.

Mrs. Fifield approved my choice—hand braided a rug for our first parsonage, tatted a dozen snowflakes for our first Christmas tree.

My mother—my son had said, smiling—*is always very quick to pray!* Not always. Not until a seventy-year-old woman taught me to go through each day looking for things for which to thank God. I think of her still as I hang white snowflakes on green trees . . . think of her, too, when I hear people say, "I'm too old to work with young people!" or "I'm really afraid of teenagers!"

Lunette Fifield was not too old, nor was she afraid to take one into her home. And she was not too timid to throw down a challenge—"Tomorrow night, Clarine, it'll be your turn to pray."

It was a challenge that changed my life.

LEARNING TO LOVE

TAOISM FOR RHYMESTERS

If you were here, sweet love, there'd be no time
For dallying with rhythm or with rime,
For tapping syllables—now which is best?
Dactyl or trochee? iam? anapest?

If you were here, sweet love, there'd be no need
For scribbling sonnets none will ever read.
We'd find a far, far better thing to do
That sounding accents, tapping two by two.

Oh, when you come, sweet love, these eager lips
Will be on yours, not pursed on pencil tips.
From dawn till dark, sweet love, sweet love we'll make,
Then sleep, and make sweet love when we awake.

Until that time, hoping to make it sing,
My foolish verse into the void I fling.

Clarine's homemade college wardrobe was weird and wonderful—like this dress made from banners for a Beta Theta Pi costume party.

"Yet Ah, that Spring should vanish with the Rose!
That Youth's sweet-scented manuscript should close!"

The Rubaiyat of Omar Khayyam

THE LARGE ROUND RHINESTONE BUCKLE

Now here in my button box is a 'rose in December'—a large round glittering rhinestone buckle that always seems to wink at me. This 'rose' has thorns. . . .

My brother Lloyd worked for the Merrill Trust Company, had just bought the family's first car—a green Ford sedan. All summer I kept pestering him to drive me up to Orono someday to see if I could go to college. One day he did.

Registrar James Gannett, grey-haired and austere, peered at me over steel-rimmed glasses.

Scholarships? No, there were no scholarships for freshmen. Bangor High hadn't given me one? I was runner-up, I told him, for the Louis Kirstein Scholarship, but John Cutler was first and he was coming to Maine on it. I could, I said, borrow the $62.50 for tuition from the Methodist Student Loan Fund. What I needed was a place to work my board and room.

Mr. Gannett peered at me again, shuffled some cards on his desk, picked up the phone.

"Caroline? . . . Jim Gannett. Have a young lady here wants to work her board and room. You looking for someone? . . . . No, she's not very old, and she's not very big." He raised his eyebrows at me. Sixteen, I told him, and a hundred and fifteen pounds—very healthy.

He passed along these vital statistics, and a short time later Caroline Bartlett was examining me with her intelligent, quizzical, no-nonsense eyes.

Arthritis, she said, touching the crutches that leaned against her rocking chair, and Professor Bartlett did all the cooking—he was a chemist in the Experiment Station. My duties would be to wash the breakfast dishes, pick up the newspapers, make the beds, and peel vegetables for dinner before I left for eight o'clock class. I needn't come home for lunch—the M.C.A. had a room where students could eat a sandwich.

She'd expect me back by five, though, at which time I'd set the table for dinner, serve it, wash the dishes, sweep the kitchen, and set the table again for breakfast. There'd be extra jobs on weekends, but I'd be allowed to go to church Sunday mornings and at

Thanksgiving, Christmas, and Easter I could go home. If I'd been assiduous in my duties, she said, I'd be given a five-dollar bill on those three holidays.

My brother thought he was driving me home in his green Ford, but I wasn't really riding with him at all! I was high in the sky on a cloud—I was coming to college!

No girl ever came with a more peculiar wardrobe. My mother, widowed only the year before and with six children to clothe, was the recipient of cast-off garments from countless charitable people— all the way from the bent, elderly ladies in the Methodist Foreign Missionary Society to the more stately, more portly, white-clad matrons in the Eastern Star. Each garment—of whatever size, style, color, or suitability—was spread out before the creative eyes of Mrs. Chadwick, itinerant seamstress.

"Can you do anything with this?" my mother would ask hopefully. Mrs. Chadwick could always do something, though what she did was sometimes wild and wonderful. For two dollars and a bountiful lunch, she would come and push the treadle of mother's Golden Oak Singer Sewing Machine up and down vigorously from dawn till dusk for as many days as we could afford to have her.

Buttercup had just calved. Mother sold Sam Goose the calf for ten dollars. Mrs. Chadwick came for five days and, humming or whistling all the while, sewed me into college.

A dance climaxed Freshmen Orientation Week. My very first dance. Which of Mrs. Chadwick's creations would be most suitable for this momentous occasion? I tried on several—unsatisfactorily, because the mirror in my bedroom at Professor Bartlett's showed only my top half. Finally I chose a little black satin number with a wide net sash that completely cupped my back side and ended on my front side at a strategic spot four inches below my navel with a three- inch round, glittering, eye-catching rhinestone buckle.

That night, as knowing upperclassmen looked over the little freshmen co-eds, I was very popular. And no wonder. Mrs. Chadwick should have been in New York sewing for chorus girls in *Ziegfeld's Follies*, not dressing naive sixteen-year-olds for a stag dance run by the Maine Christian Association. Almost every boy I danced with asked to walk me home. Of course I'd said yes to the first one—Hank Gowdy, handsome, swaggering junior at Delta Tau Delta.

Hank was delighted when he found I lived off-campus, a ten-minute walk away and with no particular curfew. When we reached the little field house by the girls' hockey field, he suggested we sit down on some bags piled alongside and wait for the moon to rise.

I pointed out to him that it was starting to drizzle, but he said he was tired and really wanted to sit and rest awhile anyway. So we sat down on the plump, stuffed burlap bags.

After a few minutes on the bags I told Hank he really wasn't acting very tired. Perhaps he'd rested long enough and we should walk along. I stood up with considerable dignity to do just that— and Hank began to laugh.

Not only laugh. Guffaw. He couldn't seem to control himself— got up off the hard bags and turned round and round, clutching his stomach. Pointing to the round white circle on the seat of his formerly navy blue trousers, I also began to laugh.

"Mine, too?" he gasped. Too? I twisted my neck, tried to see my own rear. Yes, the all-encompassing cup of black net was no longer black. It, too, was a bright white circle.

We tried to brush each other off, but that was impossible. Chalk used to mark the lines on hockey fields must be mixed with glue— viscous beyond belief. We giggled and wiggled our white rears the rest of the ten-minute walk to Professor Bartlett's house. As a matter of fact, we grinned at each other a bit whenever we met on campus for the next two years.

Hank never asked me for another date and I never wanted him to. The mental image we had of each other's bright, round, chalk-white derriere precluded any romantic feelings.

The chalk never did come out of the black net. "Whatever became of that black satin dress?" my mother asked more than once. "The one with the big buckle?" The buckle I had tossed into her button box—the dress, into the trash.

Her button box is mine now. For some fifty years whenever I've searched for a button a great, round, glittering, glistening rhinestone eye has winked at me — a thorny 'rose,' reminding me of the wasted talents of an itinerant seamstress . . . reminding me of the first real live 'college man' who ever walked me home . . . reminding me I should always look in full-length mirrors . . . reminding me of how very young we all once were.

"No, I yearn upward—touch you close.
Then stand away. I kiss your cheek,
Catch your soul's warmth—I pluck the rose
And love it more than tongue can speak—
Then the good moment goes."

Robert Browning

THREE ELDERLY GENTLEMEN NAMED JAMES—
And One Young One Called Bill

Now here are a silver punch ladle and a gold-trimmed cake plate with a handle—treasured since June 28, 1938, the day I received them. On that day Dr. James Norris Hart, Dean of the University of Maine, and Dr. James Stacy Stevens, Dean of the College of Arts and Sciences, carried plate and ladle from Orono to Bangor, put them alongside a pink vase, wedding gift of Caroline Bartlett, widow of Dr. James Bartlett, head of the Maine Experiment Station.

I cannot think of my first year in college without remembering these three dearly loved elderly gentlemen, each named James . . . without remembering along with them a young gentleman named Billy Goodell . . . without remembering two college dances, one in February, the other in March, ten years before 1938 . . . .

I am standing at the top of the stairs in Dr. Bartlett's house, waiting for the doorbell to ring, fingering pink organdy petals. I suppose every woman has at least one gown she never forgets, a gown she wore on an especially felicitous occasion, a gown in which she was particularly happy. This pink organdy dress—fashioned of layer on layer of petals, tiny ones in the cape at the top, graduating to larger and larger ones in the skirt—was such a gown for me.

Where Mother had found money for it, I don't know. Perhaps she had sold Sam Goose another calf, or even a cow. My home-made wardrobe when I'd come to Orono that fall had been weird and wonderful beyond belief. But I'd been pledged to Phi Mu, and for this first sorority formal at the Penobscot Valley Country Club, I was given twenty dollars, sent to shop at Rines. The gown had cost sixteen dollars. With the other four, I'd gone to the Bangor Shoe Store behind Freese's where Mr. Albert Schiro always gave Millie Coffin's six children a ten percent discount. For four dollars Mr. Schiro had fitted me to a pair of white satin slippers, dyed them pink to match the gown. I felt very good about myself that

February night as I waited for Billy Goodell to ring the bell.

I didn't know Billy very well—didn't know any boy very well. To get from Dr. Bartlett's house at 148 College Avenue to classes on campus, I had to walk past five fraternity houses. Often some boy would come dashing out of Phi Kappa Sigma, Lambda Chi, Delta Tau Delta to walk alongside. Billy came dashing out of Phi Eta Kappa, calling "Wait up, Sis!"

I'd told him my name, of course, but he never used it, said I reminded him of a favorite aunt. His 'Sis' reminded me of my four brothers. And we both came from sea-faring families. So when I had to invite a boy to my first sorority formal, I'd invited Billy—and been a bit surprised when he accepted.

The bell at last, and Dr. Bartlett answering it . . . .

"Come in! Come in! My, don't you look splendid!"

"Good—good evening, sir. Is—is Caroline ready? I've come to take her to the dance."

Caroline! Could it be Billy called me 'Sis' not because of some aunt but because he hadn't caught my unusual name?

"Caroline? Why, yes, she's right in here! We'll ask her!" He grabbed Bill's arm, propelled him into the living room where Caroline Bartlett, crippled long years with arthritis, sat reading the paper, wooden crutches propped on either side of her rocking chair.

"Caroline, are you ready? This splendid young man says he's come to take you to the dance!"

I gathered up my petaled skirt in both hands, took the stairs two at a time—"Dr. Bartlett, Mrs. Bartlett, this is Billy Goodell—"

Where Mother had found the money, I don't know. Perhaps she'd sold Sam Goose another calf—or even a cow.

35

pulled Bill toward the front door, Dr. Bartlett's booming laughter following us.

"Better tell him *your* name, too—Caroline!"

Billy did look splendid—brown Derby very dashing, studs in his starched dress shirt real diamonds. I was proud, indeed, when I took him through the receiving line, introduced him to the chaperones, including Dean and Mrs. Hart . . . even prouder when we began to dance.

What a marvelous dancer—especially on the waltzes! Clyde Lougee and Norman Lambert's orchestra was famous for its waltzes. Halfway through the evening we were dancing to an especially dreamy one when I felt a sharp tap on my pink-petaled shoulder. Startled, I opened my eyes. Dean James Norris Hart was looking down his long, hawklike nose at me and he was not smiling.

"Are you tired, Miss Coffin? Perhaps you should go home? We notice you've been dancing for some time now with your eyes closed."

I kept my eyes wide open after that, no matter how dreamy the waltz—and wide open, too, when we stepped out the door at the end of the dance to discover Billy's car blanketed in snow. In Maine February blizzards come up thick and fast.

"Oh, no! My pink slippers! They'll be ruined!" But sea captains' sons are nothing if not gallant. Gallantly this one picked me up, carried me high and dry through the snowdrifts to his car, and at 148 College Avenue carried me up the long walk to the house. Of course, I thought Billy Goodell was wonderful!

The next morning at breakfast I elaborated on just how wonderful he was as I told the Bartletts all about the dance. Well, almost all about the dance. I did not mention waltzing with closed eyes or sharp tapping on the shoulder.

Someone else did, though, at sometime during the day. When I came home from the library that afternoon, I was invited to sit down with Dr. and Mrs. James Bartlett for a 'conference.'

They were quite displeased, Mrs. Bartlett said, with my conduct. Not only had I invited a boy I'd picked up on the street, a boy who didn't even know my name to escort me to a formal dance, but, once there, I'd danced half the evening with my eyes closed. Worst of all, I'd let this young man carry me up the walk to their home. If neighbors were watching, they'd surely think I was intoxicated. Never under any circumstances was this to happen again. They hoped I'd learned my lesson.

"I've learned my lesson—" I wrote in my diary that February 1928 night. "Keep your mouth shut, Clarine. No one sixty-five years old can possibly understand the youth of today."

And it did happen again.

Several times I tried to teach Billy my odd name, but he never used it—went right on calling, "Wait up, Sis!" as he came dashing out of Phi Eta. In March he invited me to his spring dance.

Marjorie Buffam operated the only beauty parlor in Orono. Permanent waves had not yet been invented, but with a hot curling iron Marjorie could crimp into the most stubborn head of hair something called a marcel. The only trouble was that, as spring formals rolled around, co-eds all wanted marcels the same day. Six-thirty in the morning was the only time Marjorie could crimp me, and I had an eight-o'clock class.

She did a beautiful job, but, half-awake, took longer than usual. As I raced down the hill toward the bridge, a mile from campus, I had exactly eight minutes to make my class. Of course I tripped, fell, sat weeping beside the road, both hands around my left ankle when a car pulled up.

Dean Stevens brought a gold-trimmed cake plate: "For parsonage teas." Dean Hart brought a silver ladle: "Put a little punch in the ministry!"

"Miss Coffin? Is something wrong?" Dean James Stacy Stevens got out, commiserated, helped me into his car, drove me to the infirmary. Two hours later, my broken ankle encased in plaster, I reached Bill by phone. So sorry, I told him tearfully . . . surely hoped it wasn't too late for him to invite someone else . . . .

But Billy didn't want to invite someone else. Who needed dancing? We'd sit in his room and talk—swap sea stories. The Bartletts watched disapprovingly as once again I was carried down their long walk, my white cast stuck straight out so no neighbor would think I was intoxicated.

At Phi Eta Kappa I was carried up the winding staircase to Billy's room. There we talked the spring dance away while Phi Etas on my dance card—Marr, Brewer, Day, Cushman, Lowell, Larabee, Stetham—and a dozen others wandered in and out of Bill's room, autographed the cast, teased me about my six-thirty marcel.

Dr. James Bartlett died in 1935. I don't know if Caroline was remembering the pink organdy gown when she chose a pink vase for my wedding gift. I do know Dean James Stacy Stevens smiled as he gave me the gold-trimmed cake plate with the handle. "For parsonage teas," he said. "Don't go too fast—and God bless." And I remember well the words of Dean James Norris Hart as he handed me the long silver punch ladle: "Put a little punch in the ministry, Clarine—and keep your eyes open!" Three distinguished elderly gentlemen, each named James, each dearly loved. And one young gentleman called Bill . . . gallant sea captain's son who called me 'Sis,' who reminded me of my four brothers . . . .

The four brothers all said their last 'So long, Sis,' years ago. The young gentleman, himself an elderly gentleman now, still calls me 'Sis.' It is good to have this fifth brother . . . to answer the phone now and then and still hear a familiar, dearly loved voice saying, "Hi, Sis!"

MEA CULPA

You tell me:
"Make a little image out of wax, wax, wax
And buy a little box all full of pins, pins, pins
And every time you think of me, stick one in . . . ."

Every time . . .
>   I go for the mail
>   or cross the bridge
>   or walk in the rain

Every time . . .
>   I read a poem
>   or see the new moon
>   or wish on a star

Every time . . .
>   I meet a boy and a girl
>   walking hand in hand
>   the wind in their hair

Every time . . .
>   I glance at the stands
>   the topmost row
>   where you first said the words

Oh, I'll make a little image out of wax, wax, wax
And I'll buy a little box all full of pins, pins, pins
And every time I think of you, I'll—

Need lots and lots of pins, my darling . . .

>   boxes . . .

>   and boxes . . .

>   and boxes . . .

>   of pins . . . .

THE HAND

The hand that stopped writing
Hangs there
Over the arm of the flowered chair
In the snapshot you sent at Christmas . . .

I remember that hand, remember it well—
Carrying books,
Rifling pages, searching for sonnets . . .
'Bright Star, would I were steadfast as Thou art . . .'
At the box office, proffering bills,
Holding my coat, black velvet,
Opening doors, menus,
Tamping a pipe,
Leaning on bridges,
Lifted high, pointing at stars . . .

I remember that hand, remember it well—
Clearing the ground,
Tucking in blankets,
Picking a flower,
Touching tears,
Smoothing my hair,
Reaching for pebbles,
Waving goodbye . . .

I remember that hand,
The hand hanging there
Over the arm of the flowered chair . . .
Remember it well—
The hand that stopped writing.

UNHEALED

Strange that the wound is unhealed
after all these years . . .

that the hurt never quite goes away
never quite disappears . . .

that the heartache and pain are still there
and the useless tears. . . .

MYSELF SET FREE

Halfway down the maple tree a broken limb
Hangs on year after year, resisting wind,
Rain, snow, and ice . . . resisting time.
                                          Grotesque—
Small branches pointing down, not up—it clings
Unnatural, destroying symmetry . . . .

I think of you who loved all trees: "We will trust
Our love so long as it can bear us up."
It broke, of course—could not sustain the weight
Of separation, loneliness, cold ink—
Came crashing down, but halfway only, clings,
Destroying peace, destroying harmony . . . .

I'll call the nurseryman. He'll sever, cut,
Set free the shackled tree, leave wood for me.

I'll kneel to lay the fire, place carefully
On each dead stick a long-dead memory,
Then strike the match . . . and stand—myself set free.

41

ANALYSIS

The just man has an upright soul
But, oh, an icy breath!
He blew cold words on newborn love
And froze the babe to death.

He dragged love naked to the light
Of mind's bare atmosphere,
There to expound her raw birthmarks
Until she died from fear.

Wind her a shroud of pale white cloud
And tender wrap her round.
Carry her to some barren place
And tender lay her down.

Bury her in the early dawn—
Is she my life's last child?
Let the earth fall without a sound,
Save laughter wild.

Go from the grave with empty arms—
Tearless, turn away.
Go from the light with blinded eyes
Who cannot face a day.

"He showed me lilies for my hair
And blushing roses for my brow;
He led me through his garden fair
Where all his golden pleasures grow."
William Blake

COUNTRY GIRL—CITY BOY

A folded wad of paper sailed through the air in Professor Bailey's *Old Testament* class, landed on my open notebook. I looked around. Three rows over a pair of very intense, very dark eyes—I unfolded the wad of paper.

"Want to come for a walk after class—see the roses? Elizabeth Park's not far—a five-minute walk." I looked across again, nodded. This was Bailey's fourth lecture on the fifth chapter of *Judges*. He'd been stuck there ever since school had opened the month before. I didn't know Elizabeth Park, didn't know the writer of the note, but roses anywhere with anybody sounded like a welcome change from *Judges* 5.

"I'm getting pretty sick of that chapter," I sputtered as the tall, dark-eyed classmate led me up a hill, across Prospect Avenue. "He's been on it since September!"

"It's supposed to be the oldest part of the *Bible*." Hands in pockets, sucking a pipe, he seemed exasperatingly calm.

"So what? Who cares? I don't know much of anything about the *Bible* and that's what I came here for. When are we going to get on with the rest of it?"

"Oh, eventually, I suppose—"

"I'm seeing the dean tomorrow—dropping *Old Testament*!"

"Better not—have to have it to graduate, you know . . . See the roses?"

"Oh! Aren't they beautiful! Up around all those arches! Can we walk under them? Sit in that little round thatched house in the middle? What is it anyway?"

"It's called," he said, taking my arm under the first narrow arch, "a gazebo."

Learned a new word, I thought, *if I haven't learned anything about the **Bible**. Never heard of a **gazebo** in Maine. . . .*

We climbed the steps, sat on the green park bench. My exasperatingly calm classmate filled his pipe, put an arm along the back of the bench, began the story of his life.

"I'm twenty-seven," he said. "Cornish—" It was an interesting story, but rather long. They were serving dessert when we got back for dinner. . . .

43

Next morning I dropped Professor Bailey's *Literary Analysis of the Old Testament*—took it three years later, of course, in order to graduate. By that time I had walked under the rose-covered arches in Elizabeth Park many times, sat many times on the bench in the round thatched house called a gazebo . . . sat there most often with the same tall, dark, unruffled classmate, who, two years after the first walk, had put a diamond on my left hand.

Like all Cornish people, Jack Grenfell loved flowers. I still don't know why he loved me. He had made a firm resolve, he told me that first afternoon, never to fall in love with a schoolteacher and never under any circumstances with a woman minister. I was both—a schoolteacher for the past four years and preparing to be a woman minister for the rest of my life. Why me? Perhaps he didn't know either.

Was it contrast? Opposites, they say, attract, and we were certainly opposite. Until I'd come to Hartford, I'd lived all my life within a ten-mile radius of one small Maine city—gone to college ten miles north of Bangor, taught school ten miles west. 'Home' for me had always been the same place—a house built before the Civil War for my great-grandmother on land her mother, a Penobscot Indian, had known all her life, and her mother's forebears—who could guess for how many centuries?

Jack had lived in many homes, beginning in St. Ives, Cornwall. Son of an itinerant Methodist clergyman, he had attended school in thirteen different places, had lived in several large cities—Cleveland, Stamford, New York, Hartford, Boston. Was it naivete that amused and attracted this rather sophisticated man? Certainly he

never tired of telling our children exactly how naive I'd been that first year in Hartford. . . .

"'Do all the dogs here have rabies?' your mother wanted to know, first time I took her downtown. 'Is that why they have to be held in check?'

"What do you mean?"

"'Why, that sign! It's the third one we've passed! There's one on every other lamp post—*Curb your dog!*'"

Our children, growing up in New York City, knowing all about curbing dogs, would chortle and choke at their ingenuous mother whose dogs had run free and uncurbed through Maine fields.

"And do you know what she said the first time I took her for a ride in my car?"

"No, what? Tell us, Dad!"

"Well, Grandpa and Grandma lived in New York then. I'd been home that weekend, seen a Broadway play, and was telling your mother about it when we happened to drive past a few cows out in Avon—"

"Not 'a few cows,'" I'd interrupt. "Hundreds! The biggest herd of black-and-white Holsteins I'd ever seen!"

"Don't interrupt, dear. Well, here I am discussing lighting and staging and what the drama critics had said about this play when your mother grabs my arm! 'Look!' she yells at the top of her voice. 'Slow down! Did you see the beautiful big bags on those cows! I never saw such big bags in my life—did you see them?'"

"You never did look at the cows—only at me, with your mouth wide open! You never did see how big those bags were!"

45

"I was too astonished! I'd taken quite a few young ladies for drives by then, but no one, not one, had ever yelled, screamed, grabbed my arm, almost put me in the ditch pointing out the mammoth size of a hundred bovine mammary glands!"

"Look, Mom," our children said for years, whenever we passed even the scrawniest old cow, "did you see the beautiful big bag on that cow?"

"And do you children know—" their father would go on and on to his rapt audience—"can you possibly imagine what your mother wanted to do the first time I took her to the movies?"

They knew, of course . . . had heard many times, but never tired of hearing.

"Tell us, Dad! What'd she want to do?"

"Well, I didn't have a car then, so we'd gone into Hartford by trolley car. Your mother was all dolled up, of course. Our first real date, and she was trying hard to catch me. She looked pretty good, too, especially her feet. Highest spike heels I ever saw, even in New York. The trolley car got us to Loew's Poli almost an hour before it opened, so we walked up and down Main Street, killing time.

"After awhile I took her over to see the Capitol—only about a half-mile through Bushnell Park. Your mother said the Capitol was too gaudy—all that gilt paint on the dome—not nearly so beautiful as the one in Augusta, Maine. She was interested in a smaller building, though . . .

"What's that pretty little stone house over there?" she pointed across the Park.

"Why—er—that's a Comfort Station."

"Oh, yes, I can see it now—carved in stone right over the door—*Comfort Station*. What a nice idea! Can anyone go in?"

"Well, yes," I said. "It's for the public—"

"Then let's go in and sit down awhile till the movie opens. I could use a little comfort—kick off these shoes. They're killing me."

Twenty years since it had happened, and he was still laughing.
. . .

So perhaps that's why he fell in love with me—because I made him laugh. At any rate he was soon asking me to marry him. After about two years I said yes, he could bring a ring to Bangor in August when he came on his vacation. I had a church, but was not ordained, not allowed to administer the sacraments. I wanted Jack to baptize some babies and serve communion to my parish. In July he wrote that he'd bought the ring at Michaels Jewelers on Main Street, Hartford.

So I was to have a ring. A diamond. I spent more hours that month planning the putting on of the ring than I did writing sermons.

He'll leave Bridgeport, I thought, *the first morning of his vacation. Trip takes eight hours . . . probably get to Bangor around dinner time. Of course he'll want to take me out. Where should we go? Lucerne-in-Maine! It's just opened and everyone says it's perfect!*

We'll eat by candlelight, I elaborated the details . . . *stroll under the pines, watch the moon rise over Phillips Lake, listen to the music . . . they say the orchestra's marvelous, and they rent boats, too. Should we go out on the water? No—too risky. What if he got excited, dropped the ring? Better stay on dry land. And then—the perfect moment . . . I'll know it when it comes, hold out my left hand. He'll kiss it, of course, tenderly . . .* I looked at my hands. *Must remember to rub more cold cream on my hands . . . picking peas is ruining them. . . .*

It did not, of course, work out that way. The timetable was all wrong. I badly underestimated the eagerness of my Cornishman.

My family had been having trouble that summer with couples parking in our long driveway. It had become almost a lovers' lane. We didn't mind the couples, but our half-German police dog, Sigma, did. No sooner would a car pull in, motor and lights be shut off, than Sigma would begin a barking if not loud enough to wake the dead then certainly loud enough to wake all of us.

By late July my younger brother Millard, nineteen, had worked out a solution—each night loaded five cartridges into his hunting rifle, propped it near his window, and, the instant Sigma began barking, pointed it skyward, unloaded it into the air.

"You shoulda seen 'em last night, Suke," he told me gleefully around the kitchen table the night before Jack's arrival. "Scared the livin' daylights out of 'em! They backed outta that drive so quick you'd never know it." He pushed the fifth long red cartridge into his rifle. I wound my hair around the last of two-dozen fat wire curlers. Mother finished shelling the peas I'd spent the day picking.

"Hope they don't wake us all up tonight," I told them. "Need my beauty sleep. Tomorrow's the big night." I unscrewed the top of the cold cream jar, began rubbing my hands.

"Rub your nose, too," my mother said, "It's red as a beet. And your neck. You should know enough to wear a hat when you pick peas in the sun."

I rubbed on gob after gob of cold cream—nose, face, neck, hands. Mother pulled a flowered nightgown from the clothes basket. "Better wear my old nightie if you're going to slather yourself all over like that—save your good one."

So—bathed in cold cream, garbed in the faded flannel roses of mother's size 46 nightie—I laid my wired head on the pillow, visions of diamonds, moonlight, pines, music floating through it in spite of two-dozen curlers. . . .

Rifle shots, not music, woke me . . . Sigma's furious barking. The ten-hour trip had begun not at eight in the morning but at six in the evening, within minutes of the last parish call, and so, of course, had ended in our drive just before dawn.

Was it a bit early to knock on the door? Perhaps. Better crawl into the back seat, take a nap. . . .

He never took the nap. I jumped out of bed and looked out the window. Odd—Sigma had barked, Millard had fired, but this car, this familiar-looking car, was not backing out the drive . . . rather, it was pulling up the drive. And then I heard knocking and a voice. The voice, too, was familiar.

"Don't shoot! I'll marry your daughter!" Jack! Forgetful of all else, I ran down the stairs to unlock the door—

"Darling!" He flung both arms around me, kissed me, stopped kissing me—stuck out his tongue. "Ugh—you're all slippery!"

Only then did I remember, turn, try to race up the stairs, get halfway—

"Darling—don't you want to see your ring?" He was grabbing the hem of the flannel nightie, pulling me down on the stairs beside him, opening the black velvet box, holding under my sunburnt, coldcreamed, slippery nose the diamond ring.

"Do you like it, my darling?"

Not the way I'd dreamed it. Not the way I'd planned. No music. Rifle shots and a barking dog. No careful makeup. Cold cream and curlers. No moonlight through the pines. Faded roses on an old flannel nightie.

But I do know a perfect moment when one comes along. I stuck out my left hand.

LEARNING
TO
LABOR

" . . . my mother,
Out to buy a world for her two daughters
With her Charge-a-plate."
                              Pamela Grenfell Smith

G. FOX and COMPANY—*the big, beautiful, twelve-story store on Main Street, Hartford.*

"Her robe, ungirt from clasp to hem,
No wrought flowers did adorn,
But a white rose of Mary's gift,
For service meetly worn . . . ."

Dante Gabriel Rossetti

WE DISCOVER G. FOX AND COMPANY

'Your treasures!' Marjorie had said. "Your antiques!" An 'antique,' I understand, must be at least one hundred years old. My portable black Singer Sewing machine must be close to that. Once pushed by a treadle, it was probably 'electrified' around the time of Thomas Edison. Shall I put it in my will?

Jack paid ten dollars for this relic early in 1941 so that I could sew diapers for the coming child. His mother gave me a bolt of Birdseye diaper cloth. I sewed hard for nine months and had the proper equipment at hand when our son arrived. By the time John was seven or eight, my sewing speed had much improved.

"Ma," he'd say, pulling Bob—or Tom or Dick or Sam—into the parsonage kitchen, "will you make this kid a pair of pants in forty-five minutes? He says you can't."

I'd stop doing whatever I was doing to meet the challenge—set the old black Singer on the dining room table, push in the plug, stand poised with the scissors. John, meanwhile, would have taken Bob—or Tom or Dick or Sam—to the attic to pick out whatever rummage-sale garment was to be cut up and rejuvenated.

Our children were scavengers—very big on rummage sales, especially after the sales were over. While weary church women waited for the Salvation Army or the Goodwill truck to come clear away the left-overs, John, Lorna, and Pamela would still be pawing through the piles, still searching for treasure.

"Hang this in the attic, Ma," John would say, dragging in a large plaid man's suit, size 44. "I'll grow to it." Eventually he might have, but often he couldn't wait. Another eight-year-old would be lured into the parsonage, the forty-five-minute gauntlet thrown down, the large plaid dragged from the attic, the alarm clock placed where—elbows on the dining room table, chin in hand, eyes unwavering—two boys could watch the speedy progress of the clock's hands and of mine.

Sometimes John found a suit with two pairs of pants. This was a real prize, for it meant that Bob—or Tom or Dick or Sam—could

51

have a pair of pants exactly like his and that in only ninety minutes the two of them could march out of the parsonage, strut arm in arm down Bell Boulevard looking like identical twins.

All children want to be like other children. For ours, growing up in a fairly affluent suburb of New York City, this was in many ways impossible—never a shiny new bicycle, no elaborate jungle gym in the back yard, no Ping Pong table in a basement playroom, no flight to Florida over school vacation to visit wealthy grandparents, no sailboat on Little Neck Bay, no family yacht. Cleverly they inveigled other children into thinking it was fun to be like them— great fun to dress alike in plaid pants made in forty-five minutes on a beat-up old sewing machine from some rummage-sale left-over.

Lorna and Pamela often salvaged yards of material—cloth so ugly no one would dream of paying money for it. Skirts could be made in thirty minutes—faster than pants—and sometimes, if the cloth were ugly enough, three or even four cut from one piece. Sometimes bows could be cut to match skirts. To go pirouetting down the Boulevard with Sue and Rosemary and Cookie all dressed like them—that was real belonging. Maybe even better than a yacht on Long Island Sound.

When the family moved to Hartford, Connecticut, things got better. We discovered G. Fox and Company.

Pamela Grenfell, Peggy Presley, Joan Bormolini, Julie Wilson, and older sister Lorna in ten-cents-a-yard-taffeta skirts stitched up in thirty minutes by mother— "To pirouette down the street dressed all alike—now that was real belonging!"

52

I hope Beatrice Fox Auerbach has a wide variety of beautiful halos from which to choose in heaven. She deserves them. This small, gentle, clever Jewish lady was the salvation of many struggling clergy families. She was certainly the salvation of ours. Her ten-percent discount was given automatically to ministers, priests, rabbis. And on our monthly bill that sometimes—during college years, during weddings—ran to four figures there was never a stamped 'Please Remit.' She knew we would pay G. Fox as soon as we could. And we did.

Pamela was eight when her father began his long Hartford pastorate. Her memories of the great, welcoming, twelve-story store are a child's memories. She sent her *Hymn of Praise* from California some years after she herself had moved west, married and become the mother of a daughter. I do not know whether it is 'great poetry,' for I cannot judge impartially. I only know that it is a 'rose in December,' and that, although I have read it many times, I can never do so without tears.

SHOPPING
Hartford, Connecticut
1956 - 1964

To my mother
A hymn of praise to G. Fox & Company

On the eleventh floor, the top, they sold the toys,
And one counter sold jewelled collars, rubber bones,
And other things for pets. On the tenth floor
Was menswear, and on the ninth floor
Was womenswear. Housewares and linens on eight,
Children's on seven, crystal and sterling on six,
Formal women's on five, furniture on four,
Shoes on three, plants and more housewares on two,
And on one, where the doors let in cold air from the street,
Were jewelry, cosmetics, stationery and perfume.

And in and out of the store? Do you remember
How to get in and out? Maybe twenty doors
Revolving, opening, shutting, polished and guarded,
Front, side front, side, back, and putting you
Inside in different places—by the jewelry
Or the elevators, or the stationery and cosmetics,
Or on the second floor, or in the basement.

The basement, of course, was everything for cheap.
We went there in winter particularly for gloves—
Black kid, invisibly irregular.
The ceilings were lower than in the rest of the store.

Halfway between two and one was the mezzanine.
Only one escalator got you there.
I might ride up to two and back several times
Before I could stop halfway. The mezzanine
Sold books mainly, and eyeglasses and trips.
It was my favorite.

                    But do you remember
The luncheonette and ladies' lounge on two?
Twenty-five cents let you in to a stall with a shower.
Who goes to a department store to take a shower?
The luncheon menu was perfect and received.
I could watch people eat all day in there, each plate
Divinely fussy. But ultimately I'd stick
With the world's most completely self-assured egg salad
On whole wheat, with a cup of tea.

What happened in the store? Last and most poignant,
My older sister, a thin bundle of mysteries,
Buying French perfume for her honeymoon.
Before that, a thousand fittings, a thousand sandwiches,
And my mother, out to buy a world
For her two daughters with her Charge-a-plate.

Bloomingdale's is never so passionate, Macy's is never
So intimate, Jordan's is never so vital,
Filene's is never so aristocratic
As G. Fox was on a winter day,
Shopping for that one perfect thing.

And I dream often of wandering in the store
Looking for you to ask your permission for something
Or hiding—I didn't like to undress in stores,
And you might want me to try something on.
I look for you there often when I'm asleep.
Probably always will.

Remember the tea?
Remember the air on every floor smelled different?
Remember the circle of chairs in the ladies' lounge?
And remember the cosmeticians eyeing each other?
Remember riding the escalators straight to the top
At Christmas, when the toys glowed like a rising sun?

And what came of it all? College, and marriages,
And children and jobs, and in the closets wool skirts
With plenty of years left in them. I've been thinking
Lately of what you bought, and paying for it,
And the beauty and complexity of the store.

When I look for you in my dreams, I come to an escalator
I have never seen before. Up I go, of course,
To find new worlds to shop. There is no sign
Telling me where I am or what I can buy,
Only a small, dimly lit room where women
Examine goods on tables—nightgowns, dresses,
Blouses, infants' things—all white, all white.
Beautifully made of finest silk or cotton,
All white.

The prices! The prices are incredible!
I saw a dress for forty-seven cents!
Look at these deals! Wait 'til I show my mother!
What to do first? I pick out a few things
And wait in line for a clerk. I'll pay for these,
Then go get you and we'll set to work in earnest.
The room is cool. The women's voices are quiet.
As I wait I search for a down escalator
And think, here she can buy anything she wants.
I must find her and bring her here as fast as I can.

This is when I waken. You say you're too lame
To shop any more—come join me in my dream.
We will fill up our arms. We may never leave the store.

Pamela Grenfell Smith
Reprinted by permission

The sanctuary of South Park Methodist Church, on the Green in Hartford.

SOME OTHER, BRAVER DAY

For Jean Durham

Dull winter day . . . no sun . . . a threatening pall
Of clouds . . . a day, perhaps, to shop the mall,
To wander aimlessly . . . .
                              But don't stop there
By racks of lacy cards for those who care
Enough to send the very best. Walk fast . . .
And look the other way as you walk past
Red satin candy boxes, each a heart.
A goldfoil Cupid with a paper dart
Can make tears start . . . .
                              Don't stop to finger ties,
And smoothing rough tweed jackets isn't wise,
Nor lingering near high piles of sailing gear—
Who needs a jaunty Captain's cap this year?

Don't ask about a special blend of tea . . .
Nor pause to browse through books about the sea—
White gulls and scudding sails and surf . . . .
                              Don't gaze
At rings and things seen through a salty haze—
Easy enough to say that diamonds last
Forever when forever doesn't last . . .

Walk fast . . . look for an exit . . . down this way—
Come shop the mall some other, braver day.

February 14, 1984

The Grenfell family in 1952 when they moved from New York to Watertown—
Clarine, Jack, Pamela, John, Lornagrace, and Rebellion, the boxer.

"Sudden a thought came like a full-blown rose
   Flushing his brow."
         John Keats

"DO YOU KNOW BEEFSTEAK?"

There was only one millionaire in our Watertown church. One December the parsonage family was invited for dinner, served thick, tender, juicy filet mignon.

"We had beefsteak!" Pamela, four, rehearsing for the Christmas pageant, told her classmates in wonderment. Then, looking around at the circle of white-clad angels, "Do you know beefsteak?"

Sunday School teachers laughed, nodded, repeated Pamela's 'cute' saying throughout the parish. "She sounded," one sniffed, "as if beefsteak were the miracle, not the birth of Christ!"

In 1952 the Methodist Church in Watertown, Connecticut, did not pay its pastor a beefsteak salary. Not even a hamburg salary. Sometimes not even a macaroni-and-cheese salary. But we did not complain. We had asked to come there. The lungs of one child were badly scarred by tuberculosis. "Get away from the coast— from New York City," the doctor had said. "Up at least seven hundred feet." The altitude in Watertown is eight hundred feet. We had taken the fifty percent cut in salary gladly, moved there.

Someone who heard the story of Pamela's amazement, though, evidently thought beefsteak should not be more of a miracle than Christmas to a little girl, or perhaps that the two miracles should be connected.

The parsonage adjoined the church. Doors were seldom locked. When the family came home from Midnight Christmas Eve Service, there on the kitchen table was a large package, wrapped in the glossy white paper butchers use for meat.

"What is it?" John asked, passing it to me. "It feels heavy." I knew the feel if not often the taste of beefsteak, took it to the sink, opened it. Five thick slices of tenderloin.

"Beefsteak!" Pamela shouted. "Can we cook it right now, Mama?" I glanced at Jack.

"Why not?" he said. "It's been six hours since those pancakes." He passed me the black iron frying pan.

I turned the stove to high. "Hang up your coats, kids. Wash your hands. We'll have Christmas breakfast right now."

"Can we eat by candlelight?" Lorna's small hand was still shielding the candle flame she'd carried across the snowy walks. Her father looked at the sweet, thin face, the enormous eyes.

"Why not?" he said again.

So shortly after midnight we ate our miraculous Christmas breakfast by the light of five small candles.

We had four Christmases—'52, '53, '54, and '55—in the white church in Watertown. The Midnight Service there was always special—bells from the Episcopal Church, the Congregational Church alternating with ours to ring out over the hills the joyous message of Christmas.

Jack's service was always beautifully simple—the Story from *Luke* and *Matthew*, the singing of carols. Then in the darkened church we would approach the altar reverently, light from the Advent Wreath our own small candle, hold it high, and, singing, form around the sanctuary the Circle of Light.

> *"Glory streams from heaven afar!*
> *Heavenly hosts sing Alleluia!*
> *Christ the Savior is born!*
> *Christ the Savior is born!"*

As the five of us walked along home after our second Midnight Christmas Eve Service, Pamela, five now, was wondering about miracles . . . "Do you suppose," she whispered to her sister, "there'll be beefsteak?"

There was. The same big package on the table. The same glazed butcher paper. Jack reached for the black iron frying pan. The children set their lighted candles carefully in the middle of the kitchen table . . . .

The package was always there each Christmas we were in Watertown. No name. No card. But, as I came to know our people better, I guessed. A blush told me I was right.

'Jim' Barlow was a tall, thin, vital man, clean-shaven but as white-haired as any Santa. His youngest son, John, was in Korea during those years. Sometimes during the week I would go into the sanctuary for some forgotten thing, see Jim, head bowed, sitting in his pew. His wife, Marjorie Black Barlow, had been in charge of costuming four-year-old angels that first Christmas.

"Who's your butcher, Jim?" I asked him offhandedly one day shortly after Christmas. "He certainly cuts good steaks!" And the cheeks of our kind, loving, fair-skinned, white-haired Santa turned bright pink.

"Marj's idea," he said. "She thinks parsonage kids should know beefsteak."

And they did. At midnight around a candlelit kitchen table. For four happy Christmases in Watertown, Connecticut.

Often as I clean out cupboards, drawers, I come across the stubs of small white candles carried home from Midnight Christmas Eve Services. Not candles, really—'roses in December.'

I HAVE A SNAPSHOT

For Corporal William D. Shaw, Jr.

He won't be home for Christmas.
He won't be home again.
He's buried off there somewhere
In a place they call Saipan

Oh, other boys are coming home, coming home, coming home!
The wire is read!
The news is spread!
Cakes baked, fires laid, the windows in their room
Flung wide, and loving hands
Smooth clean white sheets
Upon their bed.
My boy is dead.

He won't be home for Christmas.
He'll never be home again.
But I've a snapshot of his grave—
It's somewhere in Saipan.

"The wind came briskly up this way
. . . set down its load
Of pine scents, and shook listlessly
Two petals from that wild rose tree."

Thomas Bailey Aldrich

SWANS IN ECSTASY

"Hey, Ma, come look! Want me to make you 'n' Dad a lamp out of this?"

"Out of those old roots? How could you ever get it to set straight?"

"Turn it upside down, of course . . . saw two or three feet off the trunk. I could make it," he added, "for your anniversary present."

It was 1958. Jack and I had been married twenty years. Since this was to be an anniversary present, we watched with special interest as our sixteen-year-old son labored over the water-soaked stump pulled from the shallow waters of the cove.

With a stiff floor brush he scrubbed away at the mud, caked deep inside each crevice . . . sawed across the trunk more than once to make an even base . . . dragged the stump indoors when it rained, outdoors when the sun shone. Eventually the dark roots dried out, took on the silvery sheen of driftwood.

Such projects were nothing new. We were always working on one thing or another to improve Nana's Camp. The eighty-foot-long log cabin had originally been built to give Boy Scouts from Bangor a 'wilderness experience.' Mother bought it in the early '40's so 'Bart would have a place to go get a deer in the fall.' Bart came in the fall, but Grenfells came in the summer. For a quarter-century we were the ones who had the 'wilderness experience' as all or part of our month's vacation was spent deep in the woods on Plantation 33, Long Pond, Maine.

The first few summers Jack had tried to revive the generator that had furnished the Boy Scouts with electricity. But Methodist ministers are not electrical engineers. Now and then he got dim flashes of light to flicker up and down the wires inside the electric bulbs strung around the camp. Finally he gave up, bought an Aladdin lamp for our fifth anniversary.

Some years later real electricity became available—wires strung from the main road through the mile of virgin forest—but Nana's Camp still had more kerosene than electric lamps. A new electric one would be welcome.

We enjoyed our primitive life on Long Pond during those powerless years because of its beautiful privacy. No radio, of course, but neither was there a telephone. That meant no meetings, no weddings, no hospital calls, no funerals, no parishioners with problems demanding the minister's attention. We rejoiced in isolation. For one month each year wife and children could have husband and father all to themselves. How wonderful!

So there was time for family projects—trees cut for a new dock, the rowboat scraped and painted bright orange, rope swings hung from tall pines, the generator house torn down and a play house built with the old boards. Everything unwanted in the five big Coffin houses on Broadway, Bangor, found its way to Nana's Camp. On rainy days the children turned the handle of my father's old Victrola, danced around the woodstove to the songs of Harry Lauder, while I, like Mrs. Chadwick before me, pushed the treadle up and down on mother's Golden Oak Singer Sewing Machine, created wild and wonderful garb for my daughters to wear back to school—P.S. 31, Sedgwick, Hall, and eventually Mt. Holyoke College. And in between projects, we swam, fished, climbed mountains, picked berries, and talked.

Especially talked. Each day ended with talk. Five rocking chairs lined the screened-in porch near the lakefront. Night after night the creak of rockers and the lap of waves mixed with the rise and fall of voices. Night after night father, mother, son, and two daughters watched the sun go down, listened to the loons call from lake to lake, took turns reading aloud from father's favorite *Lorna Doone*, laughed, teased, joked, and, just before tumbling into bed, prayed.

"Crazy swans!" "No, not crazy. Happy!"
"Very happy! Swans in Ecstasy!"

63

HOUSES OF FOUR COFFIN BROTHERS

Merle and Brity's house, 706 Broadway

Millard and Marcelle's house, 891 Broadway

ON BROADWAY, BANGOR, MAINE

Lloyd and Margaret's house, 'the old place,' 782 Broadway

Bart and Betty's house, 735 Broadway

Now the lamp project neared completion. John went with his father on the weekly shopping trip to Bangor, came back with socket, cord, a huge red shade. Impatiently he waited for darkness and, when it came, carried in the lamp, set it on the corner table, pushed in the plug, triumphantly turned the switch.

"Happy twentieth anniversary, Mom and Dad."

"It's beautiful, John!"

"Good job, son."

"Those long roots look like swans' necks," said Lorna, who has the artist's eye.

"Some swans!" Pamela laughed. "Necks all twisted around like that. They look crazy."

"Not crazy," said Father, his arm around Mother's waist. "Excited maybe, and happy. Very happy."

"More than happy." Mother searched for the right word. "Ecstatic."

"That's it! Ecstatic! Swans in Ecstasy!" We never could decide who had said it first.

And so roots were turned into swans and the lamp was named.

Since 1958 its light has shone down on tree roots that lay for unnumbered years in the muddy waters of a forest cove . . . roots dead, rotting, useless, until the creative hands of a loving son salvaged them, gave them new beauty. A hundred images come easily to mind when I turn the switch of that lamp, see its glow fall on the long grey necks of Swans in Ecstasy. I will share only three. . . .

"What's Pamela doing out there on the pine needles?" I ask Jack, who has just walked by her. "She hasn't stirred for a half-hour!"

"Oh, she's trying to get a butterfly to land on her toe."

"Did one?" He asks when our three-year-old comes in for lunch.

"Yes, Daddy. A big orange and black one."

"That's a Monarch."

"Oh—well, I've almost got a poem in my head about him. Mama, will you write it down?"

We are all in the orange boat late at night. The lake is very calm and we have rowed out to see the stars. Lorna, perhaps five, lifts a thin arm, points to Betelgeuse, low on the horizon, glowing red.

"Someday, Daddy, I'm going to climb right up and pick myself a star."

Vacation is over. There is the packed car, the loaded trailer, ready for the long trip back to the city . . . and there is John, weeping as he walks around Nana's Camp, puts small arms as far as they will reach around each giant pine. "Goodbye, old tree! Keep growing! . . . Goodbye, old tree! See you next summer! . . . Goodbye, old tree!"

"He shall be like a tree," the first *Psalm* says, *"planted by the rivers of waters . . . ."* To grow and live a tree must have long roots, must send them deep into the earth for sustenance, for nourishment, for life. And so must a family—send deep, deep roots into the rich soil of time spent together, time spent laughing, talking, sharing, praying, loving.

My tree-root lamp reminds me of this . . . reminds me, too, that sometimes to see possibilities, to find beauty we have to look at things from a different perspective . . .

"Hey, Ma, come look! Want me to make you 'n' Dad a lamp out of this?"

"Out of those old roots? How could you ever get it to set straight?"

"Turn it upside down, of course!"

"A rose is sweeter in the budde than full blowne."
John Lyly

SHOW 'N TELL

Teachers, of course, always know more about what goes on in the homes of their students than the students' parents ever dream. From the 'Show 'n Tell' hour in kindergarten right up through senior high, there are no family secrets from teachers. They know all because students tell all.

When one is teacher as well as parent in the same school system, the situation becomes even more precarious. Often I would enter the faculty lounge only to have conversation come to an immediate halt. Fellow teachers, smirks on their faces, would give each other knowing looks as they abruptly departed. Without asking, I would know that John or Lorna or Pamela had again been at their favorite sport—regaling the class with some hilarious tale about their parents.

As our children progressed through the grades, their stories more and more often took written form. Since all three had unusual verbal ability, their revelations would often be quickly entered in some local, regional, or even state writing contest, enjoyed by a dozen or more amused judges—usually teachers from other systems—and sometimes even published before either father or mother had laid eyes on them.

What our three wrote was often revelatory not only to other teachers, but also to us. Take, for example, the following by middle child Lornagrace, age fifteen. Here I thought I'd been teaching hospitality—the pleasure of opening one's home for happy occasions, the joy of entertaining friends. When I finally read Lorna's insightful story—published for all to see in the school literary magazine, awarded a Gold Key in the Connecticut Scholastic Writing Contest—I realized that I'd really been teaching hypocrisy, manipulation, and downright lying. Some 'roses in December' have prickly thorns! Let this be a warning!

'TAKE ME JUST AS I AM!'

Mother is quite a character. Father took her 'for better or worse, for richer or poorer,' but we three kids have to take her just as she is. Take, for instance, when she has a party . . . .

When Mother has a party, things begin to happen! What things? Well, just about any and every! The whole process starts when Mother breaks the news to Father. He, of course, is the last to know. Mother has a special way of doing this.

"Dear," Mom says, "one of the teachers at school is having a baby. Do you mind very much if some of the women stop by here one evening to give her a few little gifts?"

"How many?" Father mumbles, not looking up from his newspaper.

"Babies? Only one, I hope."

"No!" Father crumples the paper. "How many people—people?"

"Oh, not very many! The shower will just be for the women teachers, and you know the high-school teachers are most all men. Besides, they won't all come. They're so busy—maybe a dozen or so."

"When?" asks Dad.

"Oh, in a couple of weeks, I guess. Mrs. Carmody's leaving right after midyears—she's the one that's having the baby." Mother smiles brightly.

"Well," Dad grumbles, "I guess so—so long as it won't be too much work for you."

"Oh, I'm not going to do a thing! The women are bringing all the food. All I'll have to do is heat the water for the coffee."

Then the story follows the old pattern. The party is thought about and a plan of action laid out. This takes a few days, and then one night, after feeding Father an especially good dinner, Mother approaches him cautiously.

"Dear," she drips softly, "something has to be done about that place on the kitchen wall where the chairs keep hitting the plaster."

So Father, filled with steak, apple pie, cheese, and coffee, goes out to the garage and comes back laden with plaster, putty knife, paint, a saw, a piece of board, nails, and a hammer. Five hours and two sore thumbs later, the holes are plastered, the chair board is nailed in place, and one whole wall plus four kitchen chairs have been painted.

But this is only the beginning.

"Dear," Mother says when Father gets home from work the next day, "would you hurry over to the Five-and-Ten before six and get me three new curtain rods?"

"What do you need three new curtain rods for?" Dad pries.

"Why, silly, to hang the new curtains, of course!"

"What new curtains?"

"The ones I bought to go with the pink paint in the powder room."

"But the powder room is green!"

"Oh, I bought the pink paint, dear!" Mother says. "You don't have to bother with that. It's under the washbowl in a gallon can. Better buy a new paint brush, though, along with the rods. And some white thread."

"What for?" Father impatiently pulls on his coat.

"I think I'm going to need another spool to finish the slipcovers," she explains.

"Slipcovers?"

"They don't take long to make, you know. I'll just cut up the old ones and use them for a pattern."

"Slipcovers—thread—rods—paint—no—no—no—" Father, bewildered, but knowing how useless it is to protest, stumbles out the back door.

Now the pressure is really on. Dad paints the powder room. Mom sews. We can't even watch television in peace. As soon as we switch on our favorite show, Mother marches in with a tray of silver.

"You don't mind rubbing over these ninety forks and spoons while you're watching *Hennessey*, do you, dear?"

So the party draws nearer and nearer. Meals become simpler and simpler. Clean clothes become scarcer and scarcer. Mother becomes fussier and fussier. We aren't allowed to sit on the new slipcovers. The dog is kept outside night and day. Newspapers are spread over the fresh wax on the kitchen floor. I have to get down on my hands and knees to read the comic page in the *Times* that I was too busy to read the day before.

One day when Father pulls into the drive, a furniture truck is parked by the back door.

"One, two, three, four new chairs! What in—"

"Now, now," Mother calms him, "those old ladies have to have something to sit on, don't they? They're too old to sit on the bear rug like the kids."

"We have two dozen chairs! Exactly how many 'old ladies' are coming to this affair?"

"Well," Mother hesitates, "about thirty-two."

"Thirty-two! I thought you said—" Father can't remember exactly how many Mother said, but he's sure it wasn't thirty-two.

The night before the climax, Father is ordered out to the garage to find the old baby bassinet. Poking around on the second story in all that dust, he ruins a good shirt and loses a cufflink. Finally he struggles down the creaking ladder with the bassinet.

"It looks sort of dirty," Mother sighs, rubbing her fingers along the edge and wiping the dust on her apron. "Wish I had time to paint it with that pink paint left over from the powder room." She looks at Father.

"Well—"

"Oh, that's wonderful!" Mother chirps happily. "What would I do without you, dear? Now while you're painting, I'll put new oilcloth on the pantry shelves. Most of those teachers have never had a chick or a child, you know! Their houses are spotless!"

That night I wash two million glass cups and plates and iron five thousand pink linen napkins. They were washed and ironed the month before, but we have to do it all over.

So after we wash, dry, iron, dust, shine, scrub, wax, and generally spit and polish the whole place from stem to stern for two solid weeks, and, most important, keep it that way, what happens the night of the party? Mother always, but always, stands at the front door in her best dress and greets the guests in the following manner:

"Come right in! Come right in! But don't look at the cobwebs! Been so busy at school I haven't had time to do a thing! You'll have to take me just as I am!"

"Come right in," Mother'd say, after we'd washed, dried, dusted, shined, scrubbed, and waxed for two solid weeks, "but don't look at the cobwebs! Haven't had time to do a thing! You'll have to take me just as I am!"

"Fill the bowl with rosy wine,
Around our temples roses twine;
And let us cheerfully awhile
Like the wine and roses smile."
Abraham Cowley

THE SURPRISING THINGS THEY REMEMBER

"Put this in your next book, Mrs. G.—it's one of your best! No—
don't read it now!" A yellowed paper, faded and folded, was being
stuffed into my tote bag.

Guest of honor at the 25th reunion of the Class of 1956, Wood-
bury High, I was seated at the head table. The reunion, chaired by
George 'Buzz' Coad, Jr., was a hilarious success with class mem-
bers flying in from Texas, California. I squirmed around in my
chair, looked up at the half-dozen laughing, middle-aged faces be-
hind me. Which one? I couldn't tell. They were all 'Aggies,' and
'Aggies' had always loved to tease me.

"Remember us Aggies, Mrs. G.?" one said now. "We sure hated
poetry!"

"You practically stood on your head to make us like it," another
chimed in.

I remembered the 'Aggies,' very well, indeed—boys from neigh-
boring farms enrolled in the Vocational Agricultural School at
Woodbury High. In my sewing basket was a 240" tape measure
they'd given me once when I'd gained a few pounds. "It's to go
round the belly of a cow, Mrs. G.—multiply by five and you'll
know how much the old girl weighs!"

'Old girl,' eh . . . I was forty-five. But they'd also given me one of
my highest honors—voted me 'teacher who does most to help stu-
dents,' made me an honorary member of Future Farmers of Amer-
ica. It had been my job to teach them Shakespeare, and that eve-
ning when I stood and in a high, cracked, witch's voice delivered
the first six words of my speech—"When shall we three meet
again—" the roar of laughter from the 'Aggies' had been loudest of
all.

I remembered the laughter an hour or so later as, stretched out
in bed at the Curtis House, I pulled the yellowed paper from my
bag. *They all learned their* **Macbeth**, I thought smugly as I unfolded
the faded sheet. Then as I read, I felt considerably less smug . . .

ON TEACHING ODES ON URNS TO RELUCTANT ONES

There was a feller named John Keats
   Who wrote about a Pot.
Lord Elgin found the thing in Greece—
   Keats thought of it alot.

On one side is a mooin' cow
   A-goin' off to die
With a string o' posies round her neck—
   Keats doesn't tell us why.

On the other side's a pretty girl,
   Runnin' fast for cover,
While right behind her, pantin' hard,
   Is a feller called Bold Lover.

Some find deep meanin' in this poem,
   Dark thoughts, downright uncanny,
But I think when Keats wrote the poem
   He was thinkin' of his Fanny!

For Keats was gung-ho on this girl—
   Her other name was Brawn—
While Fanny's feelin's, like the Pot,
   Were somewhat off and on.

Keats' thoughts around this old Greek Pot
   For weeks and weeks did hover,
While Fan wished he'd get off the—subject
   And make like the Bold Lover.

Well, *'Beauty's Truth, Truth Beauty,'* Keats said,
   That's all we need to know.'
So I'll leave now and take the Pot
   Because—I gotta go.

Was this what they remembered of all I'd struggled so hard to teach—this awful doggerel? But why else had it been kept for twenty-five years? "Put this in your next book, Mrs. G.!—it's one of your best!" Then, trying to sleep, I thought of other reunions, other classes, other things remembered . . . .
   Student recollections, I find, have little to do with subject matter.

Always it is the 'affective' that stays with them—how they felt about the subject, the school, the teacher. With my students, food seems to have been a big item. They remember more vividly what they put into their stomachs than what I tried to put into their minds . . . .

"You'd bring doughnuts Monday mornings, Mrs. G.—*big white boxes of glazed, chocolate, jelly—if we'd had perfect attendance the week before. One day I went to school with a temp of 104°. The class would kill anyone that spoiled the record!*"

"*And cookies! You let us eat cookies while we read, said it kept us from moving our lips! We'd lie on the wall-to-wall with a cookie in one hand, a book in the other—*"

"*Except on Fridays—Friday was always Game Day. The girls would bring pans of brownies and we'd stuff ourselves while we played Scrabble or Probe or Password—*"

Food—and not only normal food . . . "*You'd bring big bunches of violets every spring, pass 'em out, tell us to eat a violet! That way the spring would be really be part of us!*" Dr. Kersti Ranne Linnask tells me I did this, and also that, as she obediently chewed, she'd sometimes wonder where I'd picked those violets—had there been roaming dogs?

And on Good Fridays I fed them lilacs—"*I'd bring matzos,*" Joni Rogol Segal recalls, "*because you liked them, and Good Friday and Passover often came together. We'd meet at Elizabeth Park, lie on the new green grass, munch our wafers and sprigs of lilac, take turns reading **When Lilacs Last in the Dooryard Bloomed** . . . I still love Whitman.*"

Yes, they remember food, along with other things. In Westport old junior high students remember snakes—"*The reading lab was in the basement of Old Staples, used to be the Boys' Room. On cold nights snakes would crawl out of the plaster walls and curl up in the middle of the room—little green snakes. Every morning we kids would watch while you unlocked the door, real quiet. Then you'd rush in, plunk both feet on the snakes, kill 'em dead. 'Get a paper towel,' you'd say to one of us. 'Wrap these up and go lay them on Mr. Brummel's desk.'*"

"Brummel, the principal," another says. "*Always pushin' for a new school. He'd take the snakes to Board of Ed meetings—*"

"*He got the new school! Remember the day the bulldozer came to push Old Staples down? The Digisi sisters stood there bawlin' like babies, sayin' over and over it was their high school! They must've been forty! Then they poked around in the rubble till they found two whole red bricks, carried 'em off to their car!*"

I listen to their memories and wonder . . . Carol Digisi is a superb social studies teacher, Marion the best Spanish teacher I ever knew. Do their old pupils remember the Revolutionary War, **Don Quixote** as well as they remember the tears from these 'old' teachers, the red bricks?

And can those who were in Nancy Strong Jefferson's English class in 1956 still recite '*Let me not to the marriage of true minds / Admit impediments. Love is not love / Which alters . . . .*'

"*We all learned that sonnet*," Nancy tells me, "*because you said if we did, you'd sing **Blue Suede Shoes** to the class. We did, and so you had to!*" Nancy laughs. "*You didn't know Judy Atwood had a tape recorder hidden in the front desk—we still have the tape!*"

Elvis Presley . . . his gyrating thighs had been considered quite wicked in 1956. "*Did I,*" I ask meekly, trying to recall how many hundred pounds I'd weighed at the time, "*stand up to sing?*"

"*Sure did! Swung your hips and belted it out in great style!*"

The memory is vague, but, since Nancy still has the tape, I suppose the forty-five-year-old teacher who was also wife of the neighboring Methodist minister must have done this. Did my *Letters to Seniors*, serious and dignified, make up in part for such shenanigans?

New Year's Day, 1962

And now, dear seniors, my seniors, we come at last to your year, your very special year, 1962. For you, this will be an exciting year of graduation, of going off to college—the culmination of thirteen years in public schools. During the next few months we teachers will be noting with pride signs of maturity that mean you are ready to leave the protection of home and the restriction of public high school.

We are glad to see the decreasing dependence on group approval—junior high peer pressure far behind—the increasing sense of individuality, of awareness of yourself as a person. We note that you now express with conviction the belief you might have kept silent about a few years ago. No longer afraid of being 'different,' you realize that it is your difference, your uniqueness that make you valuable as a person.

In the Honors and Academic classes I am privileged to teach, there is an increasing awareness that you need not 'follow' anyone, that you are, rather, forced to lead. Because of the gifts that have been given you, others look up to and follow you, whether you will or no. Hence you are leaders. This is a responsibility to be thought about. Your country, your world stand in great need of leaders. Especially we need unselfish leaders. Especially we need men and women of unquestionable integrity.

Lost and lonely in the midst of our gadgetry, fearful and frightened by our toys of destruction, we adults wonder where we went wrong. When did we cease putting humanity first? We need your frankness, clear-sightedness, honesty, and idealism to tell us, to set us straight. So dream your dreams and shout them to the world. Because a thing is does not mean that it is right or that it is unchangeable.

Think, too, as the spring comes on, of your responsibility to the junior and sophomore classes coming after you. It is easy, once college acceptance is assured, to slack off, to revert to childish ways. This implies that the image you were creating of yourself as a sincere, dedicated student was a false image, that you were only play-acting to get the grades, the recommendations you needed.

This year I have written something like sixty of these recommendations. Always I have given you the benefit of the doubt, said the best I could about each. Do not make me regret these fine recommendations. Maintain the image you have created of an unusually sincere, hard-working class, a class concerned with the good of the school and the community, a class willing to help those coming along after you, a good-natured class with a sense of humor, camaraderie, and kindness.

Your example is especially important in the field of English, for, as you talk excitedly about the books you are reading, the poets or novelists you are discovering, others are stimulated to read and to think. Last year hundreds of books were passed down from our library to the junior high schools—books you had outgrown, were no longer reading. This is good. Let us nourish the cultural revolution in our school, but at the same time let us avoid any superficial pretense of knowledge.

Let us never be literary name-droppers, spouting Camus, Gide, Dostoievski when all we really know about these men is their name. Rather, let us make the library a second home, take down the books lovingly, lose ourselves in them. Class work lightens after January. Reading, discussing, and thinking definitely do not.

A Happy New Year to each member of the Class of 1962! This is your year, and I like being your teacher.

> "Mrs. G."
> Hall High School
> West Hartford, Connecticut

Letters to Seniors . . . serious and dignified. I wrote them often, labored over them. But no one yet has ever handed me one at a reunion twenty-five years later, saying, "Publish this, Mrs. G.! It's one of your best!" Barbra is right certainly right when she sings '. . . *so it's the laughter they will remember.*'

Senior year—always the best year in an American public school. Here a happy Tom Kurti helps plan the Senior Prom with committee members (clockwise from center) John Coombs, Lorraine Platt, Libby Reynolds, Sally Daniels, Nancy Strong, and Class President David Jefferson.

"They are not long, the days of wine and roses:
  Out of a misty dream
Our path emerges for awhile, then closes
  Within a dream."

                                        Ernest Dowson

ANOTHER TIME, ANOTHER PLACE

"Year after year they come and fill the rows
Of seats before me—faces, rounded, square,
Dull, eager, stupid, bovine, or aglow . . ."

                            From **The Caress and the Hurt**

Thomas Martin Kurti was one of those who filled a seat before me in my senior English classroom, September 5, 1954—the day the newly built Woodbury High School opened for the first time. Built-in stage, side lights, wide windows opening on the lush Connecticut countryside—it was a beautiful classroom, and Tom Kurti's face as he entered it was definitely *'eager and aglow.'* This was his senior year, always the best year in an American public school. Tom was determined to make the most of it.

We were friends almost from the start—perhaps because we quickly discovered that we were each a bit 'different'—I, not quite like the other, younger teachers; Tom, a long, long way from the other students.

This was my first day back in a regular classroom after a fifteen-year absence spent bearing and rearing three children. Not only that. I was the wife of a Methodist clergyman and hence somewhat suspect in a public school, even though my husband's parish was six miles away in another town. Would I preach? proselytize? try to convert my students to Methodism? Already I had been ordered by the superintendent never to mention religion in the classroom. A few weeks later I would be told to omit teaching completely the few selections from the King James' translation of the *Bible* in our English anthology. *The Twenty-third Psalm* and Paul's *Essay on Love* in *Corinthians* could be downright dangerous!

Tom's background, too, was different and hence suspect. He had been born not in Woodbury village nor on a neighboring farm, but in faraway Czechoslovakia. His mother Kitti read novels in German, French, Hungarian, and there was in her American speech still a trace of her native Hungary. His father Alex, born like Tom in Czechoslovakia, was a brilliant engineer who spent his work

79

week in an aircraft plant seventy miles away. His younger brother, Frankie, was a victim of cerebral palsy.

So Tom and I were each in our own way 'different,' but, as teacher and student, we knew that we liked each other, and when one day Tom put into my hands a small sheaf of his poems, I knew that he not only liked but also trusted me.

They were beautiful poems, written during summers he had spent on Cape Cod. I was moved by them, by their sensitivity and insight, as any teacher is always moved to discover true creativity in a student. I urged Tom to submit his poems to the Scholastic Writing Contest, sponsored in our state by the *Hartford Courant,* America's oldest newspaper. He did so.

Grains of Sand won first state, then regional, and finally national recognition—the $50 First Prize for the best poem by a high school student in 1955. *Scholastic Magazine* published his poem, and, as the publication was passed from teacher to student to parent at Woodbury High School, Tom's face glowed. Never before in its long history had Woodbury High produced a national winner.

When in April we came to cast the senior play, *You Can't Take It with You,* there was only one choice for the role of 'Grandpa.' Each character in that Moss Hart-George Kaufman classic is 'different,' but 'Grandpa' is the most 'different' of all. It is he who sets the tone, the standard, for the whole Sycamore family.

Perceptive, kindly, sensitive, and always with that gleam of humor in his smile, his eyes, Tom was a perfect 'Grandpa.' No one who saw the play will ever forget his grace at the table, his 'conversation with God.' We invited a professor from Columbia University who had recently retired to Woodbury to be our critic. She wrote a glowing review, saying in part: "I came to a high school production of a great classic expecting to be bored. Instead, I was deeply moved, especially by the young man who played 'Grandpa.' "

Later Tom was in charge of dismantling the set. He postponed the task three days while other teachers in the school clamored for the use of the stage.

"Tom," I scolded him, "you've got to get your committee over to the auditorium, take down those flats, return the stage props!"

"I know—I will." He grinned sheepishly. "But I hate to take down our little house, Mrs. G. We had such a wonderful time there."

At the end of Tom's senior year there was another 'wonderful time' in a house—his own house. We were both accepted now, Tom and I, perhaps even a bit prized because of our being 'different.' I had been surprised not long before by a party at the home of Dave Jefferson, Class President, and the gift of a silver tray, inscribed *For Clarine Coffin Grenfell, with our utmost appreciation, the Class of 1955.* And when Tom invited his twenty-four classmates to dine and dance at his home after the Class Night program, the invitation was happily accepted.

Lilac, honeysuckle, weigela—the rambling white Kurti home was beautifully decorated that June night. Music from the phonograph, the grand piano, and from young voices filled the air—

> *"Though other nights and other days*
> *May make us go our separate ways,*
> *We will have these moments to remember . . . ."*

The Class of '55 sang its favorite song lustily, and a bit tearfully, as Tom, Frankie, Kitti, and Alex carved the ham, served the salads and ices with European graciousness. It might have been Vienna, and Kitti entertaining her old professor, Carl Gustav Jung. Tom—poet, actor, host—was happy that night, and, as one after another the eighteen-year-olds propelled their slightly overweight English teacher around the living room floor for half a waltz, she was happy, too.

Tom and I did not meet again after graduation. I moved to another city. Tom went on to Trinity, to Middlebury, to the Sorbonne for a wonderful year in France, to McGill. He became a doctor, prepared for a life of service. That his time of service was so brief is, indeed, tragic. But, if we count time *'by heartbeats, not by figures on a dial,'* then I am sure that three times during the year that I knew him, Tom's life was fulfilled, rich, and truly happy.

He was happy when at a school assembly he walked forward to tumultuous clapping and received the award for his beautiful *Grains of Sand*. He was happy when, again to thunderous applause, he took his curtain calls as 'Grandpa.' And he was happy when his classmates—each knowing things would never again be quite like this for any of them—filled his home with love and laughter on a June night in 1955.

Granted there were to be other joyous moments in his life—graduation from college, from medical school, hanging his shingle as M.D., the birth of his son Daniel—but the moments I have written about are the ones I myself knew and shared with a uniquely gifted student, Thomas Martin Kurti.

Auf Wiedersehen, dear Tom, till we meet again at another time, in another place—a place where you, having been there longer, will perhaps be teacher and I student.

"Mrs. G."

Reprinted in part from Foreword, *THE SEA THE LAND AND THE HEART* Verse by Thomas Martin Kurti

WOODBINE

The woodbine on the oak turned red last night. . . .

Green pointed leaves we watched in May unfurl
Wear now a braver color, twist and curl
Like scarlet ribbons round the tree's great height,
Flutter and twirl before they fall to die
Upon the waiting earth wherein you lie.

The woodbine on the oak turned red last night. . . .

. . . with our utmost devotion, The Class of 1955—*"Isn't* **utmost** *a terrific word, Mrs. G.?" Dave Jefferson asked. "Harry Hickox thought of it!"*

"I sometimes think that never blows so red
The Rose as where some buried Caesar bled."

The Rubaiyat of Omar Khayyam

BLOOD ON THE ROSES

The '60's and early '70's were years of violent death—assassination . . . years of destruction—Vietnam . . . years of deceit—Watergate. Perhaps no other single group felt the tragic happenings of these years more keenly, more sensitively than the seventeen- and eighteen-year-olds who sat, unanswered questions in their eyes, in American classrooms looking up at American teachers.

I was one of those teachers who could not answer the questions, either for students or for myself. In English classrooms, though, writing sometimes offered relief. Young people wrote thousands of verses—not poetry, but therapy for pain and puzzlement—and sometimes sent them on to the White House, to Hyannisport, and eventually to the Kennedy Library in Cambridge.

These student writings were not lacking in vivid imagery. Television screens had let them see—and having seen, who could forget?—the snarling dogs at Selma, the napalm on the villages, the bombed churches, the bodies lying on the campus at Kent State.

This is a book of memories, of 'roses in December.' Usually these memories are happy, the 'roses' sweet and fair. But not always. Teachers as well as students had unanswered questions in those days and sometimes found relief in writing. Who, having lived through November 22, 1963, could forget the blood on the roses?

TEACH US

> *"Ask not what your country can do for you.*
> *Ask what you can do for your country . . . ."*

You know now, Jack,
'What you can do for your country . . . .'
You asked, and the question is answered—
    Answered with thick thatch cradled
    in the lap of the wife and mother . . .
    Answered with laughing quip silenced forever:
    'Nobody ever asks what *I'm* wearing!"
    Answered with blood, splattering the roses . . .

And the land is splattered with tears—
Tears on white faces, hard-squeezed, reluctant . . .
Tears on black faces, unrestrained, free-flowing . . .
Tears of great sorrow and great shame
    that we, your people,
    could do this to you . . .
For one thing seems certain: we are all guilty.

As every child born in America is one of us,
So he was one of us—
    Spawned, nurtured, neglected by us . . .
    Given love, hate, indifference by us . . .
    Educated, encouraged, ignored by us . . .
We led his Scout troop, or let it die.
We taught his Sunday School class, or stayed in bed.
Our letters followed him overseas, or lay unwritten.
He was ours. Model: American. Year: '63.
    Alone, walking the corridors—
    the cruelty of our school-day cliques . . .
    Alone, planning the deed—
    the twisted mind of our deviousness . . .
    Alone, pulling the trigger—
    the crooked finger of our bigotry . . .
Father, forgive us. We do know what we do.

And you, John Fitzgerald Kennedy—
    Fighter for peace, baptized in war . . .
    Profile of courage against the mean, the low . . .
    First and martyred Catholic President—
You who believed America's greatness
    is not all in the past—
Forgive us, too, if you can . . .
    Confront us still,
    Challenge us still
    until
With deeds both great and humble we absolve
    the awful guilt of your death.
You know now, Jack,
' . . . what you can do for your country.'

    Teach us . . . .

September 21, 1964

Dear Mrs. Grenfell:

Mrs. Kennedy wants to thank the Literary Club for sending her RENAISSANCE which included some poems dedicated to her late son, Jack, the President. She is deeply touched by this tribute to his memory.

She expressed the hope that you and the members of the club will go to the Library, read and discuss the government documents, and listen to the speeches about our country's problems. Then you will understand what the President and other leaders were trying to do for the peace of the world.

Mrs. Kennedy sends to you her every good wish.

Sincerely yours,

Cynthia Stone

Secretary to
Mrs. Joseph P. Kennedy

Mrs. Clarine Grenfell
William H. Hall High School
West Hartford, Connecticut

Writing—not poetry but therapy for war, assassination, 'blood on the roses.' Often verses were sent to the White House, to Hyannisport, eventually to the Kennedy Library in Cambridge.

"There on beds of violets blue
And fresh blown roses washed in dew . . . ."

John Milton

ON OWNING A HOME

Perhaps only another nomad Methodist minister's family—moving frequently from parish to parish, living always in church-owned parsonages—can know the joy we felt in finally buying a piece of land, finally owning a home.

Year after year for nearly three decades we had come from New York or Connecticut to Maine to spend our vacation in other people's summer homes—Captain Dodge's on Isle au Haut, the Orville Trasks' on Mt. Desert, my mother's or my brother Lloyd's deep in the woods on Long Pond, Plantation 33, my brother Merle's on Lake Cathance near the Canadian border, my brother Millard's on Moosehead Lake or Surrey Bay. We knew these camps well—in Maine even the most luxurious summer home on lake or ocean is called a 'camp'—but always we longed for our own.

Finally in September, 1966, we bought from my brother Merle an eight-room house, forty acres of forest, and a thousand feet of shoreline on beautiful Alamoosook Lake in Orland, Maine. "Just pay the interest, Suke, till you get the kids through college. You can start working on the principal then."

Over the years this place, this piece of land, has come to mean much to Jack and Clarine, to their children—John, Lornagrace, and Pamela—and to the seven grandchildren—Jeb, Clara, Tamarleigh, St. John, Tallessyn, Trelawney, and Miranda. Today I watch the 'grands' skim around the lake on water skis, but I can flip back in the Log Book to the momentous day when, at four or five or six, they each received a five-dollar bill for first daring to jump off the

We love best the things into which we put our life energy.

86

Big Rock into water eight feet deep, first dog-paddled in to shore. A great day. A great accomplishment. For they knew that, once having done this, they, too, would be allowed to stay up late on the next full moon, to skinnydip off the dock, to swim that path of moonlight straight out to the waiting float.

Karl Marx was wrong about many things, but he was right about one—we love best the thing into which we put our life's energy, our physical labor. As young and old have painted, hammered, planted, trimmed trees, hauled brush, chopped wood on our forty acres, we have each come to love them more. "When I come down the side of that mountain," Lornagrace, who drives each year from Missouri, says, "all I can say over and over again is 'I'm home! I'm home! I'm home!'"

Home—a magic word. The grandchildren, part of a mobile America, have already lived in several states—some in nine, all in at least four different places. But Loon Ledge on Alamoosook Lake stays the same. When they come in the summer, they race around the camp, up and down the shoreline, through every room to make sure that nothing has changed, that everything is the same. They know Alamoosook not only as the place where they learned to swim, but also as the place where they first laid and lit a fire, first toasted a marshmallow, first feathered a canoe or rowed a boat, first caught a fish or picked a blueberry, first held in their hands a dripping white pond lily, first heard the wild loons cry, saw a snowy owl, a bald-headed eagle, a tiny humming bird, first paddled out on a moonless night and really saw the stars.

Toward the end of our first summer at Alamoosook, 1967, our son John added this verse to the Log Book. It is one of my favorite 'roses in December,' for it captures the feeling of what this lakeside home has meant to the wandering Grenfell family for nearly twenty years.

Alamoo—the place where you first feathered a canoe.

LOON LEDGE, ALAMOOSOOK LAKE

I think sometimes the night is best
   before the hearth ablaze
   to hear the dark wind-waves, whistling thrush
To find Fire Fairies leaping on the logs
   to the tune of **Memory**
   in tap-dance crackle time
To wander back a thousand years through warm winds
   pushed through the pulsing pipes of Ithaca
   into **Faith of our Fathers**—
   cosmogeny of hymns
   rocking in what time?
To wonder . . . what small foot has found
The unseen twig on the black ground?
   O lèave me, leàve me startling sound
   back a thousand years, a thousand midnight thoughts,
   a thousand memories I thought I had forgot—
   but had not . . .
I think sometimes that night is best
   at Alamoosook Lake.

But then again—
   Yes, then again when morning comes
   when the sun rides up
The wet red water highway to the sky
   when my heart fills with thanks, specific
   for this time, this place, this life
Then again—
   Yes, then again I may decide that morning's best—
   before day is really born
   before time's watch is wound
   before all fills with world-sound
   all before . . .
All before the wind and wave join shore to shore
   to smash night's glassy memory
   resting now on brow of sea
Before bees buzz, winds whisper, trees talk
Before ant walk wakes beast and bird and kin
Then best and least is when the world begins
   at Alamoosook Lake.

But you know, too—
  Yes, you must know, too—
There is a comfort in busyness
  in playingness
  in workingness
Yes, you remember, too—
When singer sings, hammer blows, oven bakes
  When broad oars dip and swing
When the whole warp and woof of working summer play
  wraps like a wide warm blanket on the day . . .
You, remember, too—
  you have known the awefilled sense:
Appropriation / protection / belonging / purpose!
You, too, have felt their awefilled grip
On eye and ear, on hand and lip . . .
  reaching down, unbidden
  to the heart, to home . . .
O yes, you've heard the lunchbell on the lake
  when grace is spoken, broken is the bread
  when beds are made without a thought of bed
  when work and play blend in unthinking sunshine
  in happiness
  in family
  in purposive beauty of life and earth . . .
It's not unusual to find
In back of mind in midday times
The hiding thought that this is best
  the times when life's with purpose blest
  times when there is no time to think
  of the great Other waiting over the hill
And over many hills where the same sunshine
  seems not to shine . . .

Perhaps you, too, have thought with me
That there are times when evening's best
  when work is done and rest begins for the rest . . .
  evening breeze, pipe, chart, and tea
  and sunset on the silver sea

The quiet leaf—still falling
   but not yet . . .
The noise of thought—we think—forgot
We think no time but evening could be best . . .
   no time but evening now that it has come
   to Alamoosook Lake.

You know,
It's not quite not caring . . . but
It's not quite caring too much.
It's not quite forgetting . . . but
It's not so sweet as child-thought ought to be
   at least in memory.
It's neither,
   nor is it in between
   nor here
   nor there
   nor anywhere but elsewhere . . .
Elsewhere from caring, like a foggy night . . .
But I'm sure you, too, remember the time
When the crack of doubt grew wide in the mind . . .
   wide, wide in time . . .
   when you wonder which is the picture-frame
   and which the picture true of life . . .

And the only clue that God will make
   to the quiet cry of the night-thought prayer
   to the chilly still of the midnight air
The only clue that God will make
   is the lone loon's cry, high over the lake. . . .

John Millard Grenfell
Loon Ledge, Alamoosook Lake
1967

LEARNING TO LOSE

AFTER THE DREAM

I keep my eyes closed a long while
       after the dream . . .
       not wanting to lose you
       not wanting to let you go . . . .

I keep my eyes closed a long while
       after the dream
       remembering your face
       young, vulnerable
       wet with tears
       cradled in my shoulder . . . .

I keep my eyes closed a long while
       after the dream
       willing you to stay
       willing you not to leave me . . . .

It's the 'ecstasy of victory' all the way as Bedford Junior High 1979 champions lift their adored Coach Hall high in the air.

"Each noon a thousand Roses brings, you say;
Yes, but where leaves the Rose of yesterday?"

The Rubaiyat of Omar Khayyam

"COURAGE, PAL!"

September 5, 1929, was my first day of teaching school—Hermon High, a tiny two-teacher school ten miles west of Bangor, Maine. I was eighteen, the salary $850 a year. Out of this affluent $23.66 weekly stipend, I paid Mr. and Mrs. Russell Patten $5.00 for board and room. The only other expense was for skis and ski poles. The road past Pattens' farm was sometimes the last to be plowed, and we two teachers were expected to be at school on time.

My last day of teaching was March 23, 1976—Bedford Junior High, Westport, Connecticut. I'd been a reading consultant in Westport for twelve years and did not want this to be my last day—wanted to go on till 1979, round out a full half-century. But knees that at eighteen had flexed and bent and skied easily up and down Maine hills were stiff and arthritic at sixty-five, could barely carry me from car to desk.

From touching corridor walls for support, I'd regressed to a cane, to crutches, and finally to a wheelchair. Since Christmas Dr. Glenn Hightower, principal and friend, had met me each morning at the parking lot with the wheelchair from the nurse's office, pushed me to my reading lab. At the end of the school day, he or someone else would push me back.

Westport is a superior school system, confident enough of itself to be lenient, humane, kind to an older staff member. But teaching from a wheelchair was breaking all the rules, even breaking state law. What if there were a fire? Teachers were supposed to help children get out, not vice versa. In February I'd handed Glenn my resignation.

"Promise you won't tell anyone," I'd said. "Farewells, pity, commiseration—that I can do without." He'd promised.

"You didn't, did you?" I asked the morning of March 23 as he pushed the chair down the long corridor.

"Didn't what?"

"Tell anyone?"

"You asked me not to, and so I haven't—no one."

"Thanks, Glenn."

He unlocked the door of the lab, flipped on the lights. "I wanted to," he said, his hand on my shoulder. "Wanted very much to give you a party, a grand send-off. But I understand . . . have a good

95

last day, Mrs. G." I wheeled the chair further into the lab, looked around . . . .

Red geraniums in bloom on every window sill. Charlie Boyle, science teacher, always brought them from his garden in September, kept them blooming through the winter . . . . On two walls wide shelves filled with paperbacks, magazines, tapes, games— Probe, Scrabble, Password. Al Wakeman, custodian, had built the shelves for me. My classes were small, never more than twelve. Around the room were twelve bright aqua carrels, each with its controlled reader, tape recorder, head set . . . nearby the tachistoscope, record player.

I thought of my first reading lab in Old Staples—the converted Boys' Room, always on rainy days the slight smell of urine, a few dozen tattered paperbacks, and snakes. I thought of annual budget requests labored over. Would the Board of Ed approve this? Could we afford that? Here finally were all the materials I'd ever asked for, all any teacher could need to help students improve their reading. Here finally . . . .

In the middle of the room was a ten-foot-long walnut table, given by the Board for the faculty lunch room when the whole staff had numbered only twelve. My small classes had loved sitting around that table—reading plays, talking, reaching into the cookie jar in the center, playing 'Dummy Chair.' I'd certainly miss that old table! Twelve years . . . forty-seven years . . . last day . . . .

"Hi, Mrs. G.—here's your coffee. Hey, where's that smile?"

Since the wheel chair, Coach Edward Hall had gotten in the way of bringing me coffee from the teachers' lounge each morning. "Where's that smile?" he asked again, then gently, "Is the pain bad today?"

I reached for a tissue. Coach Hall knew me very well, was hard to fool. I didn't even try. I needed a teacher just then—not an administrator, not a principal, but someone who knows what it is to work every day with kids, to love kids. I needed another teacher.

"It's my last day, Coach."

"No! Your last day? You've resigned?"

"A month ago. Asked Glenn not to tell, and he hasn't." I pulled another tissue from the box. "Don't you, either. I couldn't take it." A bell rang. Students poured into the room. "Promise?"

"I promise . . . courage, pal." He went off toward the gym.

'Pal' . . . that he was, and had been since my first day at Bedford. It had been an odd friendship. Except that we each had a happy marriage, one son, two daughters, no two 'pals' could have been more unlike, more different.

Old—young . . . female—male . . . northern born, Maine— southern born, Florida . . . one-time Protestant minister, now a minister's wife—devout Roman Catholic layman . . . overweight, slothful, pale, an indoor person, physically able to do almost nothing—lean, trim, finely muscled, tanned, an outdoor person, physically able to do almost anything . . . .

Why over the past twelve years had Coach so often invited me to ask the blessing, give the invocation, at Sports Banquets honoring his players? Was it because, hurrying to a football game that first fall, I'd taken a short cut through the locker room, opened the door to see sixty boys in spanking white uniforms all on their knees as their coach prayed?

"Separation of church and state, eh," I'd teased him after we'd won the game. "God's been kicked out of public schools, hadn't you heard? You'll get yourself kicked out, too." Was that why I'd so often been asked to come pray? Or had it been simply to show those lithe young boys and girls what an unexercised, undisciplined body could become?

Coach's body was, of course, a model of fitness—quite literally a model, for Westport artists and photographers called on him often to pose for movie posters (Ed Hall's body, Burt Lancaster's head), for book covers (the football player on *Brian's Song*), for packages (the bowler on the *Wheaties* cereal box). Students liked to look at the pictures of different military uniforms in *Collier's Encyclopedia*—British, American, French, Nazi. The uniforms, the beards and moustaches were different, but they knew all those military gentlemen were really their Coach—

And here he was again, coming into the lab with a tall, green-paper, florist's cone in his hands, setting it carefully on my desk.

"For you," he said, "for courage. No, I haven't told anyone—except God. Stopped at the church a few minutes." He hurried off, turned back at the door, yelled over the heads of the entering twelve-year-olds, "Why don't you remind these nitwits how to spell *embarrass*?" I laughed, as he'd known I would, and pulled the green paper off the pot of tall yellow tulips.

"Do you remember," I asked the class, "how to spell *embarrass*?"

"How could we forget, Mrs. G.? But show us again! We like to see you do it!"

"I can't stand up. You'll have to show me."

With one accord they jumped to their feet, turned their backs to the wheel chair, laid one hand on each buttock, slapped hard on the double *r*'s and double *s*'s.

"Not single, but double," they chanted in unison." Not one *r*, but two *r*'s. Not one *s*, but two *s*'s.

"Very good. Now spell it."

"*Em-barr-(Slap! Slap!)ass-(Slap! Slap!).*" Then, as loud as each could yell, *"EMBARRASS!"*

Giggling, exhausted, they fell back into their seats. "Can't spell it as well as you, Mrs. G.," the boldest shouted. "Don't have so much to slap!"

"That's right, Charles. Now stand up and tell me how you spell *accommodate*?"

"Well, I'm too young—so *you* say, Mrs. G.—to go out alone with a girl, so I hafta *double* date—Charlie and Clarabelle—only I don't know any girl named *Clarabelle*! Gosh, whatta name!—anyway, Charlie and Clarabelle have to double date with Melvin and Myrtle."

"Good, and what does Clarabelle say when Charlie puts his arm around her? Does she say *e* or *i*?"

"No! She says '*O*,' and so does Myrtle."

"Spell it for me, class. All together now—"

"*ACCOMMODATE—A-Charlie-Clarabelle-O-Melvin-Myrtle-O-out-on-a-double- DATE*"

I'd been teaching a class how to spell these two words my first day at Bedford. I'd known almost nothing about teaching reading, except that poor spelling and weak phonics often go together. So I'd given a spelling test, explained mnemonics, and been standing back to the class, hands on my own broad buttocks, slapping vigorously, when I heard too much giggling behind me. I'd turned, seen a handsome young man, immaculately dressed in white slacks, blue flannel jacket, standing in my doorway. He'd grinned at me, waved, gone off.

"Who," I'd asked the still-giggling class, "was that?"

"Coach Hall—"

"We were alike in only one way—a happy marriage, a son and two daughters." Coach Edward M. Hall, his wife Barbara, son Edward Jr., called 'Gator,' and daughters Melissa and Stephanie.

That noon in the teachers' lounge Coach Hall had put his tray down next to mine, put both hands on the back of the immaculate white slacks, slapped vigorously.

"I will never," he'd said, looking down at me, "so long as I live forget how to spell *embarrass*. May I sit here?"

"I was a little worried," he'd told me near the end of that first lunch, "when I heard they'd hired a minister's wife to teach my boys—you'll have lots of football players—but you'll do just fine, Mrs. G."

So we'd been friends—from first day to last. And that day, too, passed swiftly—Friday, Game Day. I reviewed the silly mnemonics, remembered always because they were a bit naughty, played the last game of Password around the walnut table, passed out the last cookie . . . looked at the yellow tulips when courage faltered.

I held the potted flowers in my lap as Coach Hall pushed me down the long corridor for the last time . . . past Mary Murphy, my neighbor across the hall for a decade—"Have a good weekend, Mrs. G." . . . past Mary Sprouse, bright and cheerful at her secretary's desk—"Lovely tulips, Mrs. G.—spring's here!" . . . past Barbara Arnold in the library—"That book you ordered came in, Mrs. G.—I'll save it for you." . . . past a dozen youngsters at their lockers, grinning at me, winking at Coach—"Only way to go, Mrs. G.! See ya Monday!" I held the tall tulips higher and higher in front of my face as the wheel chair rolled along the corridor and out the door of my last school for the last time.

"Courage, pal," my friend said once again, setting the tulips carefully on the floor of the car. "Can't tackle the turnpike on a Friday afternoon with tears in your eyes. . . ." He came around the car, leaned in the window.

"I've been thinking, Mrs. G.—you might try swimming. West Hartford has a great pool, and you'll have time now—"

I turned the key. "Thanks, Coach, for everything. Couldn't have made it without the tulips—and the prayer."

"God bless, Mrs. G.!"

I swam in Cornerstone Pool, West Hartford, almost every day for the next four years. After some months I could do without the wheel chair, then without the crutches, finally, except on icy walks, without the cane. At the 50th reunion of the Class of '32, six years later, I even danced a few waltzes.

And for several autumns now the knees have been supple enough to kneel down on the ground, plant brown bulbs. They blossom each spring, tall and golden yellow.

Yellow—color of the sun . . . color of warmth and friendship . . . color of courage. People admire my garden, call these flowers tulips. I sometimes call them 'roses in December.'

ALL THINGS WITH EASE, WITH GRACE

For Dr. Theos Langlie, with remembered affection

He was a man who did all things with ease—
Slalomed down mountain slopes, lobbed balls, swam seas,
Lovingly caressed piano keys . . . .

He was a man who did all things with grace—
Losing, showed the same insouciant face
As when, nonchalant, debonair, he took first place . . . .

Counselor, teacher, husband, father, friend—
He was a man on whom all could depend,
Fulfilled each varied role until the end . . . .

When Death said, "Come, sir! Play a set with me!"
He dropped the racket—easily, gracefully
Leaped the net into eternity.

April, 1983

"Rose leaves, when the rose is dead,
Are heaped for the beloved's bed;
And so thy thoughts, when thou art gone,
Love itself shall slumber on."

Percy Bysshe Shelley

THREE ECUMENICAL ANGELS AND ONE CHERUB

"And the Lord appeared again to Abraham while he was living in
the oak grove at Mamre. This is the way it happened: One hot sum-
mer afternoon as he was sitting in the opening of his tent, he sud-
denly noticed three men coming toward him. He sprang up and ran
to meet them and welcomed them . . . ." **Genesis 18:1-2.**

Jack Grenfell was the most ecumenical of men. Always he tried
to bring people together, making no distinctions—intellectual, so-
cial, racial, religious—among them and counting among his friends
those of every color, every faith, every academic or economic level.

I think of Father O'Neal of St. Mary's parish, Bethel. This young
priest often rang the bell of our Methodist parsonage to get down
on the floor with our two-year-old son, play with Tinker Toys,
build with blocks. I think of Rabbi Jerry Malino, who looked so
much like Jack that when the two of them—wearing black clergy
suits, black Homburgs, white clerical collars—walked down Dan-
bury streets together, they were often taken for brothers.

I think of Joe Klein whose corner luncheonette on the Green ad-
joined South Park Church. Joe could always be counted on to
lend—without question and without interest—any extra dollars
needed for a tuition payment at Drew or Mt. Holyoke. "Don't
worry about paying it back—whenever you're able." I think espe-
cially of Rabbi Abraham Feldman, spiritual leader of majestic Tem-
ple Beth Israel, Hartford.

Photographs of three men hung on the wall of Jack's study: his
Cornish father, the Reverend Thomas Grenfell; Rockwell Harmon
Potter, Dean of Hartford Theological Seminary during our years
there; and Rabbi Feldman.

This Rabbi was a phenomenal man. Older than Jack, he had
been counselor and friend during my husband's years at Hartford
High School and Trinity College. For many years they lost touch.
Then one day as Jack, on his way to a new charge, walked the aisle
of a Hartford-bound train, Rabbi Feldman looked up from his
newspaper and said without a moment's hesitation, "Hello, Jack
Grenfell." Their renewed friendship—not as counselor and stu-

dent, but as co-workers for the same God—was rich, real, and much enjoyed. I can see the Rabbi waltzing at the 25th Anniversary Tea Dance our children gave us at South Park. I can hear him saying as we rode in a car with him once past the many Protestant and Catholic churches in the capital city: "See all the little synagogues! How that Jewish idea has caught on!"

Jack Grenfell—an ecumenical man. So perhaps it was not accidental that at his sudden and unexpected death, the Lord sent to minister to me three ecumenical angels—a Catholic nun, Sister Margaret; a Protestant teacher, Helen Moore; and a Jewish student of some twenty years before, Nancy Slonim Aronie. With Nancy came a slender, dark-eyed cherub, her eight-year-old son, Daniel. These three angels, unlike Abraham's, did not come together. Their visitations—and ministrations—were spread out over eight days, from a Wednesday to a Wednesday. Not until the final day, the second Wednesday, did I recognize them for what they truly were . . . .

SISTER MARGARET

The clock was striking six as I picked up the phone. The eight-party country line running through a mile of woods to our lakeside camp was busy. I did not recognize the voices.

"Excuse—excuse me . . . This is Mrs. Grenfell on—on the lake . . . I've just come home and found—found my husband on the floor. He's very cold . . . I'm afraid he's—he's—"

"It's all right, Mrs. Grenfell. This is Sister Margaret at the Hermitage. You hang up—"

"But I need to call a doctor—I—I don't know the name of a doctor—"

"I'll call a doctor. You hang up now so I can—"

"But our camp is way down in the woods—you don't know where—"

"Oh, I know your camp, Mrs. Grenfell. We sisters often walk there in the fall. You hang up now . . . we'll be there in a few minutes."

They were there in a very few minutes. "This is Dr. Devlin—you come with me." The doctor knelt with a stethoscope. Sister Margaret took both my hands, pulled me up. At the kitchen table, my hands still in hers, she closed her eyes, began the Catholic Prayer for the Dead. After awhile I stopped sobbing, listened to the words.

". . . there is rejoicing in heaven tonight over a faithful son who has come home . . . there is joy in heaven . . . there is joy among the angels . . . great joy . . . ."

On Saturday in the little Methodist Church on the Narramissic River, Sister Margaret—beautiful in the bright blue habit of her Order, her face calm and radiant—read the words of the Twenty-third Psalm:

"Yea, though I walk through the valley of the shadow of death, I will fear no evil, for Thou art with me. Thy rod and Thy staff they comfort me . . . ."

Again as she left the church, she held my hands in hers: "Don't be sad, Mrs. Grenfell. He has gone to the God of Love, to the very heart of Love. How can he love you less? He loves you more!"

I did not see Sister Margaret again, for not long after she was moved by her Order to a new assignment. I think of her often, though, as I drive by the churches with the cross on top—think of her and hear her voice, calm and confident, saying the words: "There is rejoicing in heaven over a faithful son who has come home . . . . How can he love you less? He loves you more!"

"This is the way it happened: One hot summer day . . . ."

This is the way it happened: Wednesday, at six o'clock on an eight-party country line . . . a Catholic nun, Sister Margaret, just happened to be the one talking . . . .

HELEN MOORE

The Protestant angel was not a stranger, but an old and dear friend. I knew Helen Moore first as a fellow student at University of Maine in the early '30's; knew her again from 1956-1964 in West Hartford, where at Hall High she chaired the math department and I the English; knew her once more in the '80's as a fellow retiree to our native State of Maine. Jack and I had spent the last day of his life as guests of Helen and her brother Newman in their Mt. Desert Island home, fifty miles from our lake.

That last day was an especially happy one. Born and reared on the Cornish coast, Jack loved to be near the sea. He enjoyed the ride around the Island, the boats, the lighthouse, the surf at Thunder Hole, the view from Mt. Cadillac. He especially enjoyed the luncheon at Seawall where, after teasing the college-girl waitress unmercifully all through the meal, he compensated by leaving an extravagant tip.

He did not enjoy the fact that none of us, stuffed with lobster, would order dessert. He wanted his favorite, Cherry Jubilee.

"I'll make you a Cherry Jubilee," Helen laughed, "the next time you come down—pour on a whole cup of brandy and let you light the match!"

Helen did not make Cherry Jubilee in her home. She made fish chowder in mine—came early Thursday morning, as soon as she heard, stayed until the Saturday services. She came, as all Maine women come to a house of death, bearing food—homemade bread, muffins, a huge haddock not many hours out of the cold Atlantic. She made gallons of fish chowder and then, since she and I were the only ones to eat it, filled container after container for the freezer. She answered the long-distance phone calls, ordered flowers, and on Friday, my arthritic knees not holding me up, pushed a wheelchair through the Bangor Mall until I found a simple black dress.

Except for Helen, I would have been alone these three days. We had retired from Connecticut to Maine only a month before, knew few townspeople. The local clergyman was on vacation. John Nason, who cares for our grounds, came one night with a casserole his wife Lorna had made. There was no one else. Our daughter Lorna was in a Missouri hospital, recovering from surgery; our daughter Pamela, faraway in California; John, our only son, busy in his Guilford parish seventy miles north, would return Saturday to deliver his father's eulogy.

So it was good to have with me an old, old friend—someone who had known me for fifty years, known Jack for twenty-five, known my mother and my Coffin brothers . . . someone who knew our children and our grandchildren.

It was good to have with me a Maine woman, born on Gott's Island, who came with few words but with helping hands, love, and understanding . . . with homemade bread and food from the sea. It was good to have with me those three long sad days Helen Moore, no-nonsense, down-to-earth Protestant angel.

". . . rest yourselves under the tree; and I will fetch a morsel of bread, and comfort ye your hearts . . . ."   Genesis 18:4-5.

NANCY SLONIM ARONIE and DANIEL

Alone all day the following Monday, I was sitting on the dock when I heard a noisy car clanking down our hill, heard a young voice call:

"Hi, Mrs. G.! You always said to drop in if I ever got to Maine! Well, here I am, and Danny with me!"

"Nancy! Danny!" Hands outstretched, I walked up from the water. "Welcome to Alamoo!"

"You're sure it's OK? We aren't interrupting? Where's the Reverend?"

"He—he's not here right now." If I told her, I knew, she'd be quickly gone. "Danny, bring your bag and follow me. I'll show you your room." I knew Danny, had given him a reading lesson or two in Connecticut.

"Can I go swimming before supper?"

"Of course, if your mother—"

"Supper— " We were in the kitchen now. "You're alone here! Shall I go back and pick up some food?"

I flung open the door to the freezer. "What's wrong with real Maine fish chowder?"

Danny toasted marshmallows for dessert, then, stuffed and exhausted, climbed into his bunk. Nancy and I sat on by the fire, talked about writing—hers and mine. We'd each been published recently, she in a newspaper, I in a religious magazine

"Remember journalism class?" she asked. "You stuck a pad of blank paper in front of me and said, 'Write!' I astonished myself! I never knew I could write!" She picked up the religious magazine. "But when are you going to get your stuff published where Jews can read it? They'd never see this!"

"I don't know, Nancy—think maybe I'm too old."

"Don't be ridiculous! Edith Hamilton never published a word till she stopped teaching at Smith! And then see what she did—*Age of Greece, Age of Rome*— what was she? eighty? ninety?"

"Well, I'm almost seventy . . . but how did you happen to drive to Maine, Nan? Today, I mean—I've been inviting you for twenty years."

She hesitated. "I'm not sure—was tucking Dan into bed last night and the idea just popped into my head. 'How'd you like to go to Maine tomorrow?' I asked him. 'Just the two of us! We could visit Mrs. G.' Joel objected—car's so old he was sure we'd never make it! But we did! Is it really all right?" she asked again.

"It's more than all right, Nancy. I'm delighted to have you. What do you want to do tomorrow?"

"Why—Bar Harbor, of course—doesn't everyone? Climb Cadillac! Eat lobster!"

I looked into the fire. Could I do this—so soon? Do over again things done the week before—with someone who did not know? with an ebullient young woman, a laughing child on vacation? But perhaps—if not now, then never . . . .

"Bar Harbor it is, if that's what you'd like—only we won't climb Cadillac—we'll drive up. Takes younger knees than mine to climb mountains!"

The child made it easier—questions, giggles, riddles, jokes. We rode around Ocean Drive, listened to the surf at Thunder Hole, looked through the telescope on Cadillac at the small islands, the bay alive with sails. We even ordered lobster at Seawall where the college girl, remembering the tip the week before, anticipated every need.

On the way home, Nancy stopped, bought cheese and cream, made for supper what she called 'Jewish quiche.' The next morning she was up early—jogged ten miles, swam, packed her bag, but after breakfast lingered by the fire.

"Hate to go, but we must get on the road. Promised Joel we'd be home tonight, and I'm not sure we're going to make it. Danny, give Mrs. G. a hug and put our bag in the car."

"Bye, Mrs. G. I had fun—" Danny's skinny arms felt good around my neck. He did not know, but he had been substituting for seven absent grandchildren whose hugs, jokes, and laughter would have been very comforting just then. Even his mishaps, the mistakes all children make in strange houses, had been welcome — the look of fear followed by relief when forgiveness was quick and real.

"Goodbye, Danny. Come again—"

"The only bad part," Nancy stood up, "is missing Reverend G.—when will he be back?"

"Sit down again for a minute, Nan. I want you to read this before you go—" I pulled the long newspaper column from my pocket, handed it to her. She looked at the headline, the picture . . . then, startled, looked at me.

"No—it can't be! Why—why didn't you tell me?" Her eyes were full of tears.

"You would have felt you ought to leave, Nancy, and I very much needed you to stay. It happened so suddenly . . . you don't know how wonderful it's been, dear—being with someone who thought he was still alive!" She wept, of course. Nancy cries easily. And I wept with her, the first time in three days.

"Now you must really write your books," she said as she climbed into the old car. "You'll have time—and publish them where Jews can read them!" She gunned the clanking motor that never should have started out in the first place, that broke down completely a hundred miles south and had to be rescued by Joel.

She waved goodbye, and then, halfway up the hill, this Jewish angel slowed, hollered back through the open car window: "And don't dare say you're too old! Remember Sarah!"

I laughed, went into the camp, took down Jack's **Old Testament**, turned to *Genesis*. Sarah had laughed, too, I remembered, had thought she was too old . . . .

"And the Lord said unto Abraham, Wherefore did Sarah laugh, saying, Shall I of a surety bear a child when I am old?' Is anything too hard for the Lord? At the time appointed I will return unto thee . . . and Sarah shall have a son." Genesis 18:13-14.

Sarah bore her son, and I have written my books, publishing them where anyone who wants may read them . . . because the same Lord who sent three angels to Abraham long ago sent three to me—a Catholic nun, to speak eternal verities; a Protestant teacher and friend, to comfort and sustain; and a Jewish student, young and full of hope, who came with a giggly cherub to point me away from the past toward the future . . . to remind me that, like Sarah, one is never too old . . . that nothing is too hard for the Lord.

Nothing is too hard for the Lord . . . Abraham's Lord . . . the same Lord.

It is good to know that He is still around.

TRELAWNEY'S PRAYER

I thank you, God,
that Talli is my friend,
so when I lose at the game and have to cry
a little
and go in the bathroom and lock the door,
she comes
*and knocks on the door and says, **"Lawni, don't cry!***
It's only a game! Unlock the door! Come out!"

Dear God,
I know it's only a game, but just the same
I'm glad
that Talli is my friend
and comes
and knocks on the door
and comforts me. Amen.

Guilford, Maine
Valentine's Day, 1981

"Then glut thy sorrow on a morning rose,
Or on the rainbow of the salt sand-wave."

John Keats

LETTER TO SEVEN GRANDCHILDREN

July 9, 1980

I have just come up from swimming in the lake, the first time I've swum since your Grandpa died a week ago today. Of course, I was thinking about him and about all of you as I swam around the Big Rock, flopped over on my back, looked up at the blue Maine sky. You remember how, since he stopped swimming himself, Grandpa always worried about us when we were in the water or out in the boats. I kept looking up at the deck, expecting any minute to see him standing there and hear him calling down to me, "Now don't go out too far!"

Have you learned the *Apostles' Creed* yet? There is a phrase in it, *"I believe . . . in the communion of saints."* The word *saint* in early Christianity meant anyone who belonged to the church. I have always liked that phrase, and I do believe in that communion. My father died when I was fifteen, and often through high-school and college years I felt him near me, right up to the time I married your Grandpa and another strong, good man came into my life.

Somehow I feel that Grandpa has not yet gone very far away from Alamoo, that he is staying here, close by, until he's sure I'm all right and perhaps even until you all come next month to swim in the lake again. At any rate, I seemed to hear his voice inside my head and heart this beautiful July morning—clouds white and

109

puffy, water clear and warm, leaves barely stirring, white gulls swooping low—hear his voice, saying, "Now be careful, dear. Don't go out too far!" So I didn't. Please don't worry, mothers and fathers, about my swimming alone at Alamoo. I'll be 'just fine,' as John always says!

Your Grandpa was a superb swimmer when I first met him. He had been a counselor at Camp Jewel, a YMCA camp in West Swanzey, New Hampshire, for five summers. In 1935 I'd brought another minister that I thought of marrying—I was always partial to ministers—from Connecticut to Maine and taken him to the lake with my brothers and their wives, but this minister had turned out to be a real pain. When everyone else was out swimming or fishing or waterskiing, he just wanted to stay in the cabin and neck. If you don't understand that now, you will someday. So when I wrote home from Hartford Seminary in 1936 that I was bringing another minister to camp, my brothers were disgusted. They bought several gallons of apple cider and all through supper right up to bedtime kept filling your Grandpa's glass and urging him to have more.

We slept in double bunks, all in one room, and Grandpa was put in a top bunk, with a wobbly homemade ladder to climb on. Do you know how apple cider affects the digestive system? Your parents will explain. Poor Grandpa! Polite, wanting to please my family, he'd drunk glass after glass of strong apple cider. Now, all night, time after time, he had to climb down the creaking ladder, try to find one of the flashlights the boys had carefully hidden, fail, creep out in darkness, feel his way along the path through the woods—we often saw quite wild animals there, including Maine black bears—until he came to the little Chic Sale hidden in the pines, a good long distance from camp. Meanwhile the brothers and their wives, wide awake but pretending to snore and sleep, buried their faces in pillows to smother giggles.

This 'city-slicker minister from New York City' got even the next day, though. He stood for awhile on the dock, watching our novice swimming—none of us had ever been to a real camp or had a real swimming lesson—while my brothers kept urging him in. They hoped, of course, he couldn't swim at all, like the fellow I'd had the summer before, and were planning on ducking him good. "Come on, Jack! Don't be afraid! It's not very deep!"

After awhile Grandpa walked to the edge of the dock, did a beautiful dive, and swam sixty or seventy feet underwater before he came up, shaking the long black hair out of his face and grinning at us back near the shore. We were open-mouthed. We'd all been afraid he'd drowned. My brothers had been taking deep breaths getting ready to dive in and hunt for the body! Your Grandpa—he was a tease. And I can just see Jeb or St. John pulling a stunt like this at some girl's camp a few years from now.

Tamarleigh, Tallessyn, Trelawney, do you remember the tape of *How Great Thou Art!* that you made when you were here Memorial Day weekend? Grandpa loved to hear you sing that hymn, especially the last verse which you sang all together:

> *"When Christ shall come with shout of acclamation*
> *And take me home, what joy shall fill my heart!*
> *Then I shall bow in humble adoration*
> *And there proclaim, 'My God, How Great Thou Art!'"*

Do you all know what *acclamation* means? It means praise. God said to Jesus at His baptism: *"This is my Beloved Son, in whom I am well pleased."* Another acclamation is *"Well done, thou good and faithful servant."* I do not know what acclamation greeted your Grandpa at his death, but I feel sure Christ came with one, for your Grandpa was a 'good and faithful' man, serving God all his life with heart and mind and soul and body. He had great faith that each of you—his seven precious 'grands' whom he took such joy in baptizing as children of God—great faith that each of you would be the same, 'good and faithful servants' of God.

Do you, too, believe in *'the communion of saints?'* If you do, I'm certain you'll feel your Grandpa's spirit close to you many times in the future—when you win those prizes and awards, when you graduate from school, and especially in those high and holy moments when you join the church, when you take your first communion, when you choose your life companion, when you see your first child. I hope each of you will remember then that your grandfather loved you dearly and that you brought him great joy and pleasure during the last twelve years of his life. You do not all bear his name, and the three who do will doubtless change it at some future time, but you are now and always will be Jack Grenfell's beloved grandchildren.

Family and friends said goodbye to Grandpa in the little white church on the Narramissic River in Orland . . . Clara's church, where Grandpa baptized you, dear, our oldest granddaughter, in 1971 . . . where Grandpa and I two weeks earlier had sat together in the pew and worshiped . . . where he himself on the Sunday before his death preached his last sermon. His topic that morning was *Seeds*. "Look out the windows!" he told the people. "See what God has done with seeds!" Then he went on to speak of the seeds that we are, you and I, the result of someone's planting, and then of the seeds that we ourselves plant as we go through life.

I thought of your baptism as I sat there at Grandpa's funeral, Clara, and of how joyfully your Uncle Eliot, Miranda's father, had played on the organ that day the two hymns we Grenfells love best to sing—*Joyful, Joyful, We Adore Thee* and *All Creatures of Our God and King*. Your baptismal day had been a happy one, a 'time of grace,' Pamela called it. I thought of Summerfield Church on Staten Island, where Grandpa christened St. John and the three T's, of Trinity-Boscobel in Buchanan for Jeb, and of Harvard Epworth in Cambridge for our darling Miranda.

I thought of all those joyous times our family had celebrated together. And this day, too, July 5, 1980, was a time of celebration—the celebration of a life well lived. That is what a funeral means to Christians, for we believe Jesus spoke the truth when he promised eternal life. We sang the same hymns, loud and clear, that day:

> *"And thou, most kind and gentle death,*
> *Waiting to hush our latest breath,*
> *O praise Him! Alleluia!*
> *Thou leadest home the child of God,*
> *And Christ our Lord the way hath trod.*
> *O praise Him! Alleluia! Alleluia! Alleluia! Amen!"*

That is Saint Francis' hymn, you know, and he is my favorite saint. Your Grenfell parent learned all seven verses of that hymn rowing around in the old orange boat at Long Pond, Maine. Your Grandma, you all know, is never content with doing only one thing at a time. She always has to be doing two or three or even, like Julius Caesar, seven. So when your parents were children, they never just rowed and fished and enjoyed the hills and watched the sunset and dragged dirty clothes in a pillow case behind the boat to get them clean. They also memorized hymns. These are your hymns, too, so learn the words and sing them loud and clear.

I can see two loons on the lake now. Out near the island a white sailboat is tacking. The breeze has stiffened as it always does in the afternoon. I am going to close this letter, take it over and mail it to you. From time to time I shall write you others. There are many more funny stories about your Grandpa that you might like to know. He was, as you know, a very funny man.

Come to Alamoo whenever you can. Bring your friends. I plan to take good care of myself, diet, and get thin, so that I can dance at each of your weddings! Now wouldn't *that* be funny!

Lovingly,
Grandma Granfell
Alamoosook Lake
Orland, Maine

"There is a garden in her face
Where roses and white lilies grow."

                                        Thomas Campion

TWO CRANBERRY-GLASS VASES

I was watering my plants, thinking about the letter from Marjorie Freer in the morning mail. "Have you seen an attorney yet?" she'd written. "Made your will? Decided who's to have your treasures?"

I looked around the room. What treasures? Did I really have things worth seeing an attorney about? I added water to the two vases on my window sill, picked a dead leaf from the German ivy . . . well, I certainly treasured these cranberry-glass vases! Beautiful, rare in themselves, they were more beautiful, more rare because of the person who had given them to me. . . .

From 1973-1976, the last three years of my teaching, I had bed-and-breakfast five days a week with Margaret Flint, widow of Herbert Flint, on River Lane, Westport. Weekends I drove seventy-five miles to West Hartford where, after his early retirement in 1973, Jack and I had bought the old parsonage at 612 Fern Street.

I was sixty-two when I went to live with Margaret . . . thought I knew almost all there was to know about living. I was wrong. Ten years older than I, slender, white-haired, forthright, it was Margaret who showed me I didn't know very much at all. She herself had mastered the art beautifully, Thoreau style.

"A man should take care," Henry David once wrote, *"not to be thrown off the track by every nutshell or mosquito's wing that falls on the rails."* Like Thoreau, Margaret Flint was *'suspicious of any sort of purposeful activity'* that cut into her time. Especially she was suspicious and utterly contemptuous of women who devoted their total life energy to housekeeping. She herself paid it no mind whatsoever.

Margaret was good for me. Much of my life energy had been spent on housekeeping—fixing up, painting, decorating, making draperies, curtains, slipcovers, sewing sometimes straight through the night. My sin was pride. Methodist parsonages often needed much, and I hated being pitied, hated the condescension with which wealthier parishioners often passed along to the minister's family their cast-off furnishings—sagging mattresses, scratched pianos, lumpy sofas. Always I struggled—and made husband and three children struggle along with me—to make a good appearance, to 'put my best foot forward,' as Maine people say.

Margaret cared not one whit about appearances, about which foot was forward. She liked weaving and so, of course, had twelve looms. She seldom vacuumed carpets, but she once spent days weaving a beautiful green rug for the living room of my oldest granddaughter's doll house. She liked doll houses. I'm not sure how many she herself had in various rooms of her house because I never got to walk through all the rooms in her house. She liked yard sales, and some rooms were inaccessible—crammed full of interesting bric-a-brac, purchases made over a forty-year span. Margaret often gave away things, but she never threw away anything.

She was fussy only about her beds. Summer or winter she hung sheets on outdoor lines where stiff breezes from Long Island Sound either froze them stiff or whipped them dry. Then, as carefully as though they were linen tablecloths, she ironed them. After a day of teaching, I was always glad to lay my arthritic bones between Margaret's clean, smooth, sweet-smelling sheets. But aside from beds, all other housekeeping chores at River Lane were 'nutshells and mosquito wings' that, if bothered with, might easily de-rail one from real living.

Real living was keeping track of ducks, migrating geese, lordly white swans—the constantly changing wild life on the Saugatuck River, twenty feet from her windows. The appearance of one or two cygnets was cause for rejoicing and endless hours spent with binoculars. Dawns were important, and sunsets. Clouds, wind, rain, snow were all duly noted. Margaret's weather predictions were invariably more accurate than those of the TV forecasters with their charts, arrows, and whirling radar sweeps. Drama and music were important—always a season ticket at Westport Playhouse, always records and time taken to listen to them.

Despite continuing battles with foraging chipmunks, planning the annual garden was important. Days were spent leafing through seed catalogs. And not only seed catalogs. All written words were of supreme importance. This erudite lady had earned her B.A., with Phi Beta Kappa honors, at the University of Kansas, her M.A. at Columbia, and had taught English on the college level for four years. So weekly trips to the library were important.

Newspapers and magazines were important—the antiques section of the *Newtown Bee*, the cartoons in the *New Yorker*, the *Letters to the Editor* in the *Times*. Her memory was phenomenal. She'd been gone from Kansas for fifty years, but now and then she'd still find in the *Letters* a familiar Kansas name. "Bowersock," she'd say. "Julian Bowersock . . . now he must be related to the Bowersock Flour Mill in Lawrence."

The weekly crossword puzzle in the *Times Magazine* was usually conquered in an hour or so on Sunday afternoon, but many other books of crossword puzzles lay on and around the numerous dictionaries. Etymology was a passion. Sometimes, unable to think of exactly the right word for a verse, I'd ask Margaret's help over breakfast. While I spent my day at school, she'd spend a good part of her day poring over dictionaries—*Oxford, Webster's, Funk and Wagnall's, Thorndike-Barnhart*, and a dozen others. Over a cup of late-afternoon tea by the fire, she'd enlighten me.

Cups of tea by the fire, conversations about words—these were important. And news of children—'Had a letter from Jim,' she'd say. 'He's going to France with Kissinger.' Or 'Marg and Charles have decided to take his sabbatical in China—want me to come over.' Jim, suave and sophisticated Yale man, was a career diplomat with the State Department. While Jim traveled the world, Elizabeth, his pretty wife, taught diplomats' children and with a steady hand reared five Flints. In Arizona 'Marg' and Dr. Charles Nugent, professor of medicine at the University, were rearing three Nugent grandchildren.

These grandchildren were a fascinating lot. Meeting them was like running into an animated edition of Lovejoy's *Guide to American Colleges*. Some mornings when I came downstairs, a half-dozen sleeping bags would be rolled up in the hall, a half-dozen young people drinking coffee around the dining room table. Everyone liked Margaret's coffee. She simply boiled a pot of water and threw in a handful of grounds. The young people obviously liked their grandmother, too, and, like her, had their values straight. They cared not a whit about either appearances or housekeeping.

"This is Sarah—she wanted to be a vet but settled for people." Sarah, I learned, was halfway through an M.D. program at University of Arizona . . .

"And this is Daniel, Sarah's brother—" Daniel was earning his Ph.D. at University of Chicago . . .

"You met Stephen the day you came—" Yes, I remembered Stephen. Bearded, blue-jeaned, he'd been chopping firewood for his grandmother, left a few days later to study for a doctorate at London School of Economics. He'd also been collecting data for a book on rock 'n roll. Now, I learned, the book had been published, and Dr. Stephen Nugent was teaching anthropology at London School of Economics.

In 1976 I retired from Westport Schools, left River Lane. Five years later I came back to stay with Margaret while I worked for five weeks as a reading consultant. James, a Flint grandson, carried in my bags.

"Did you finish at Juniata, James?"

"Oh, yes—just got back from two years in the Peace Corps—Africa."

Margaret, leaning on a cane, greeted me at the door. She had suffered a slight shock, lost some mobility. I had recovered some mobility, lost a husband. Margaret did not like to be touched, but I hugged her anyway.

"Now tell me about the other Flints," I said as we sat by the fire. "It's wonderful that James is here taking care of you . . . Did John finish at Yale?" Yes, and an M.S. from MIT. He was staying on there, researching lasers.

"And Gretchen? How about her bar exams?" Oh, Gretchen had passed her bar exams, was an assistant professor at New York Law School.

"William was at Earlham, I remember—" Well, William didn't care much for Earlham, but they were all proud of him—just been made a lieutenant in the Bethesda-Chevy Chase Rescue Squad. Had she written me about Edward?

"He went to Kenyon?" Yes, Phi Beta Kappa—working now for his Ph.D. at University of Illinois—teaching chemistry.

Margaret filled my teacup for the third time.. I looked around the crowded room . . . February, but the Christmas tree was still up, was never taken down till Valentine's Day . . . looms, doll houses, books from floor to ceiling, Beethoven on the piano, piles of *New Yorkers*, interesting virtu from a hundred yard sales. Outside, I knew, were the tall larch trees, the piles of firewood, the boats pulled up alongside the dock, the gulls circling over the river. Was it Maria Montesorri who first taught the importance of a live environment for gifted children? How much, I wondered, had days and weeks spent in this place with this uniquely gifted, eclectic grandmother contributed to those Ph.D.'s, those brilliant careers?

"I'm paying you for my room, Margaret."

"Three nights a week? You don't need to at all."

"I insist." Margaret never liked to be given money directly. Each Monday I laid the fifty-dollar check on the dining room table when she was not around.

Five weeks later when I came down to breakfast on the last day, one end of the table was piled high.

"Sorry, dear. James lifted this stuff down for me. An antique dealer is coming this morning. I have to get rid of some of my junk." She picked up a celluloid doll. "You'd never believe what he's paying me. Five dollars for this—I'm sure I didn't pay more than a nickel."

"You have some lovely old things, Margaret. But are you selling your cranberry vases?"

"Oh, I have so many—" She picked up a vase—lovely rose glass, a silver ring around the top. "He says these are worth ninety dollars."

"I'll pay ninety dollars for them, Margaret—gladly."

"You'd like these?"

"They were always here, on the ledge of your dining room windows. How many mornings have I sat here watching the sun shine through that pink glass, drinking your coffee? Yes, I'd love to buy them." I wrote the check, laid it on the table.

"I'll stop by later for my bags, have a last cup of tea before I start for Maine."

Except for a somewhat battered shoe box, wound round and round with stout cord, the dining room table was cleared when I came back. James put my bags in the car as we drank our tea. At the door Margaret passed me the box.

"Your vases. I've packed them in newspaper—better not unwrap them till you get home."

"Thank you, dear." She did not like hugs, I knew, but I gave her one more anyway. "I'll put them in my east window . . . they'll catch the morning sun."

The shoebox rode beside me the four hundred miles to Maine. There I cut the cord, carefully unwrapped the newspaper, lifted

Treasured for their beauty, treasured even more because of their donor . . . "Set them in an east window to catch the morning sun."

117

out the rose vases, shining and clean, their silver rings brightly polished. Underneath was an envelope inscribed 'Clarine.' I opened it.

Six checks—five for fifty dollars each, one for ninety, a small white card. 'I don't want money, dear. It has been a great joy to have you again these few weeks. Come back whenever you can. Love, Margaret.'

My treasures . . . I look at them again—morning sun shining through cranberry rose glass, green ivy leaves falling over silver rings. Shall I put them in a will? Do I have a granddaughter who loves swans and clouds and dawns and words? who knows that weaving a small rug for a child's doll house is far more important than vacuuming a big one? who has *a grand suspicion of any sort of purposeful activity* that might cut into her time?

Time . . . precious time . . . the time God gives each one of us for living . . . .

GOOD MORNING, TEACH!

Each day we find in our mail at school
Dittoed copies of some new rule,
Addended, amended with long explanation—
We have a strong administration!
It's very efficient. We'd certainly heed 'em
If we ever had time to read 'em.

Westport, Connecticut
1964 - 1976

"I have forgot much, Cynara! gone with the wind,
Flung roses, roses riotously with the throng,
Dancing, to put thy pale, lost lilies out of mind . . . ."

Ernest Dowson

PEOPLE — THE MOST CHERISHED 'ROSES'

Especially for the Class of '32

So far as I can remember, I received only one spectacular bouquet during college years—a dozen long-stemmed American Beauty roses sent by Hal Ellis, '29, whose Phi Kappa Sigma pin I'd been wearing a year or so. Hal had graduated two years before and was an electrical engineer for Westinghouse down in Springfield. He was earning, I suppose, perhaps thirty dollars a week and so even in depression days could well afford the extravagance. The roses were delivered to Balentine one February day in 1931, soon after semester grades came out.

This was my first semester back after a year of teaching school. College seemed a cinch. At Hermon High the other teacher, Edgar Crozier, had taught the math and science and coached the basketball. My assignment had been to teach second- and fourth-year French, first- and third-year Latin, first-, second-, and third-year English, and girls' phys ed . . . also to coach the plays and minstrel shows, play for square-dancing during the hour-and-a-half lunch break, direct the orchestra, and organize a PTA.

Now there seemed to be all the time in the world. Since I'd saved enough money to live in the dormitory, I didn't even have to waste time 'working my board and room' at Professor Bartlett's. Whatever anyone asked me to do, I did—accepted the presidency of Pan-Hellenic, of Phi Mu, was a varsity debater and captain of the

		Orono, Maine, *Sept. 16* 1930 ,		
Receipt No. 1721		Received from *Carine M. Coffin*		
		Student's Full Name		
Registration No. 1451				
			Home Address	
Meal Ticket No.	Student's Accounts: Tuition		62	50
	Board and Room		31	25
Freshman Week Meal Ticket No.	Term Bill			
	Total Student's Accounts		93	75
	Military Deposit			
	Key Deposit			
University of Maine Frederick S. Youngs, Treas.	Special Athletic and Health Assessment		6	25
	Breakage Card No.			
per	Special Examination			
	Total		100	00

UNIVERSITY OF MAINE TREASURY DEPARTMENT

119

"People are the most cherished 'roses'—especially those one knew when one was young. Clarine (8th from L., Row 2) was invited to read from **The Caress** *and the* **Hurt** *at this Golden Reunion of the Class of 1932, June 7, 1982, University of Maine.*

Rifle team. (My brother Merle said, "If Suke can't argue 'em down, she shoots 'em.") Friday and Saturday nights I danced happily up and down fraternity row with a dozen different boys. Sundays, just as happily, I traipsed up and down the State of Maine with deputation teams, preaching the gospel in small white churches for Cece Fielder and the Maine Christian Association.

Dabbling in any and everything, I was more than a little surprised when grades were published, phoned Hal ecstatically. I knew I didn't deserve straight A's. When the long white box arrived, the same day as an invitation to Phi Beta Kappa, I made a firm resolution to stop 'fooling around' and study harder.

Nearly fifty years later Hal Ellis and his wife Lucille, now of Sun City, California, came to Alamoosook Lake. They were guests of honor at the last dinner party Jack and I ever hosted together, June 26, 1980. Roses were all in bloom that June day, and Jack had clipped some for the table. As Hal watched me arrange the centerpiece, I wanted to ask if he remembered other roses sent to Orono half-a-hundred years before, but I refrained. It would not have been tactful. He and Lucille had been married only a week and were in Maine on their honeymoon.

Though Hal's were the only roses I was ever given by a Maine man during college years, since then and especially during the last four years of widowhood, my classmates at University of Maine have given me many—loving, kind, thoughtful, considerate things done for me as I travel around the country reading from my books.

Truly it is people—not things, not flowers, not even roses—that make up the most beautiful bouquets. Those I knew and loved when I was young, especially the members of the Class of 1932, are my most cherished 'roses in December'. Now and then the Alumni Office asks me to write them a letter . . .

Dear Classmates:

This is not going to be a short, impersonal letter. Only the Sears End-of-the-Month Clearance Sale and the *Reader's Digest* Sweepstakes in my mailbox today, so who needs short? And after fifty-six years of knowing each other, who needs impersonal? So—long and personal!

Like a few others, halfway through college I stayed out to work for a year and so changed from Class of '31 to Class of '32. A seeming hardship then, but now—. . . now when I pick up the *Bangor Daily News* and see a pix of a half-dozen students cavorting around Bud Humphrey's Big Black Bear at the foot of the Mall—

. . . now when Bill Hathaway writes: "You're on TV out of Michigan City? If you get anywhere near Kalamazoo, let us know!"—

. . . now when Ray and Jo Wendell give me their almost first edition of Jack London's **The Turtles of Tasman** containing his poignant essay, *The First Poet*—

. . . now when on a speaking tour in Northern Aroostook, I'm hosted by the McIntires for a week, taken to swim in their lake September 15 (brr!), then warmed by Smith's stalwart coffee made in an old black pot over a campfire, fed Charlene's luscious Swedish coffee bread—

. . . and when Smith, pointing across the lake, says, "That's John Doyle's place over there," and I remember the red Chinese pajamas I bought for Colvin Hall's first Pajama Party in 1931 because handsome John Doyle, Phi Gamma Delta, was my date—

. . . or when Jim Bates writes: "If they don't invite you to read your poems, Mary and I will rent a hall, sit and listen all afternoon!"—

. . . or when on a swing through Connecticut Herb and Phyl Trask (who was Jack Grenfell's classmate at Hartford High) take me to lunch at posh Farmington Country Club, urge me to 'keep on writing'—or when the Jenkses welcome me to their beautiful colonial home on Tolland Green and Bob makes his special apple pie for dessert while Mickey has me read to her club—

. . . or when Ralph Prince sets up three dates in Ohio for me to speak to some four hundred people and Edna throws a crown-roast-of-pork dinner party for twelve with less fuss than I make a peanut butter sandwich—

. . . or when, driven off the Maine Turnpike by a blizzard, I toast my toes by Flo and Lin Elliott's woodfire, Lin backs my car around the snowbanks the next morning, and I go off fortified by Flo's special wheat germ-grits-brewers' yeast-bran breakfast cereal—

. . . or when on a lonely night I can dial Mollie Rubin Stearns or Louise Beaulieu Van Stack or any one of a dozen other '32 widows like myself, just to talk—

. . . or when someone from the Butlers' Bangor church invites me to speak to their Co-Weds and I say, "That's Ash Wednesday. Do you want a religious program?" and she says, "Oh, no! Be light and funny! Paul and Kay say you do that so well—

. . . or when Harland Leathers, back last year for the first time, writes from Virginia: "Wonderful to see you all . . . Jean thrilled with the way the Class welcomed her!" Or Hazel Sparrow Russell, with whom I roomed a year at Balentine, writes soon after Weldon's death: "Love your book . . . I empathize." Or our dear Win Libby writes from Florida: "The one overwhelming emotion which comes to me from reading this latest book of yours is that you and your husband had a wonderful life together."—

. . . now, when all these and many other caring and affectionate interchanges come my way, as I know they come to all my classmates, then I am very glad, indeed, that depression poverty back in 1929-30 forced me to teach school a year and so made me a member of the Class of 1932—an unusual class, a very special group of people. Open that old *Prism* and read page 43:

"Determined from the start to typify the biggest thing that ever happened to the University, we chose Paul Butler for our temporary Class President—"

Nothing temporary about Paul. He's still in there pitching, and so are many others. I think of them each time I drive by the football field and see those foot-high letters on the press box: *CLASS OF 1932*.

And what about you, dear classmate? Are you still in there pitching? Not long ago I worked alongside Aldy Denaco on a University Phonathon. "Can't spell worth a darn tonight," Aldy kept mumbling as he filled out 'Comments' on the cards after each call. "How do you spell *arthritis*? . . . How do you spell *paralyzed*?"

I thought of Tennyson's *Ulysses*—*"We are not now that strength which in old days / Moved heaven and earth . . ."* but, Tennyson has the old warrior go on, *". . . that which we are, we are!"* I thought of classmates who have come to our reunions using canes, walkers, wheelchairs. I thought of a prayer written for older people by my son, the Reverend Dr. John Grenfell:

PRAYER OF MANY YEARS

Heavenly Father,
May the years of our age be the sweetest of all.
May we neither leave our dreams behind,
Nor let our hopes grow cool,
Nor fear to look ahead,
Nor let the fires of the spirit die,
Nor the winter of the body chill the eternal springtime of the heart.
Help us to love and cherish the very best from life—
No matter that the years fly,
No matter that much of the world we knew has now gone by.
And may old age always be just a few years older than we.
Amen.*

* Reprinted from *Women My Husband Married*

And if you can't come back? If you're feeling remote from and somewhat cold toward your Alma Mater? I know the cure. Send along a gift. For years when our children were growing up and being educated, I didn't. Hate to think of all those years with nothing but zeros after my name. Couldn't I have spared five bucks? Even a small gift would have been better than a zero!

Now, with fewer demands, we try to make up. The University was very good to me, and I have never been ashamed of the education I received there from men and women whose names now are only on buildings. It bothers me very much that today's faculty at Maine is 48th on the nation's salary scale—two states from the bottom. Are we really that poor?

Over the years many classmates have been more than generous. They know well the joy that comes from giving to and even sacrificing for an institution that has been meaningful in their lives. If you don't, then send a gift. Designate it however you like—Class Fund, Senior Alumni, Libby Scholarship—but I absolutely guarantee that as you lick the stamp, you'll feel both closer to and warmer toward your college. *"Where your treasure is, there will your heart be also . . . ."* or have I got that backwards?

This June discover the joy in *giving* back, and, if you've never been, the special joy in *coming* back! We really want to see you!

With affection and all good wishes,
Clarine Coffin Grenfell '32

Roses hand-quilted by Edna Prince of Miamisburg, Ohio, form the backdrop for Clarine's reading at University of Maine, June 8, 1984.

THINNING RANKS

We keep looking around
        for the ones who aren't here . . .
Where's Milt? He always comes back . . .
        and that nice little man,
Laura Merrill's husband—Alvin,
        that was his name. We talked a long time last year . . .
And Sully, walking fast in his tennis shoes,
        young and slim and always smiling . . .
Has anyone seen him? Or Zottoli? Who'll
        tell the stories if Bob's not here?
And where's Louise, blonde and beautiful,
        dancing in Winston's arms?
We keep looking around
        for the ones who aren't here . . . .

THE WARM NEVER QUITE GOES AWAY

The old lady walks,
leaning heavily on her cane,
from Fernald, where the bookstore used to be
past Carnegie, where the library used to be
to Balentine, still a women's dormitory . . .
drops her cane, sinks gratefully to the lowest granite step,
draws a deep breath,
lets the breeze lift her hair
lets the April sun warm her. . . .

Girls, arms full of books, come and go
from class, to class, chatter, laugh,
leap steps, two at a time . . .
Now a girl and a boy come along,
he carrying the books . . .
They pause . . . he leaning against the rail,
she on the topmost step,
not wanting to leave each other,
talk, laugh, are silent . . .
look deeply into each other's eyes . . .
let the breeze lift their hair,
let the April sun warm them. . . .

The old lady listens to the silence, turns.
"Would you like to hear a poem?" she asks.
Startled, they glance for the first time
at the bundle of clothes on the bottom step . . .
faded eyes, wrinkled skin, wooden cane . . .
relic from another world
breaking into theirs.
They look at each other. The boy nods.
So the old lady tells them a poem
about a boy and a girl
who walked one day
from Fernald when it was still the bookstore
past Carnegie when it was still the library
to Balentine, the women's' dormitory
and how they, too, paused on the steps,
reluctant to leave each other,

talked, laughed, and were silent,
looked deeply into each other's eyes,
let the breeze lift their hair,
let the April sun warm them . . .

"Did you marry him?" the girl asks into the silence.
"No —" the old lady grasps the rail, pulls herself up. "No—he
    married someone else."
"Oh —" They look again at each other. Can it be love does not
    last forever?
"And did you?" The boy, wanting to get it straight, reaches
    down, hands her the cane.
"Marry someone else? Yes, I did, too."
Then, seeing disappointed faces, the old lady smiles.
"But the warm—the warm never quite goes away."

"But earthlier happy is the rose distill'd
Than that which withering on the virgin thorn
Grows, lives, and dies in single blessedness."
William Shakespeare

A FIVE-MINUTE WALK

"Want to come for a walk after class—see the roses? Elizabeth Park's not far—a five-minute walk . . . ."

This was a five-minute walk that lasted forty-five years. For sixteen of those years the Grenfells lived within a mile of Elizabeth Park. Often we would pack a picnic basket, take the children to eat supper in the gazebo.

"Now I want you to know—" my husband would say as they unpacked sandwiches, sat on the green park bench—"that this round thatched house we're in is a gazebo. You can sit down in here, even kick off your shoes if you like. But this is not a comfort station. The comfort station's over there on the other side of the pond . . ."

And over the heads of our children, intense dark eyes would be probing mine—the woman minister he was never going to marry, the schoolteacher to whom he'd once taught a word, asking if she, too, remembered the first walk to Elizabeth Park, the first time she'd sat on that same green bench, listening to a story. . . .

Always teasing, always laughter during those forty-five years. "We had so much fun," parishioners often wrote after we'd left a church, "when you and Jack were here." Teasing and laughter and fun and roses. Sometimes the roses were part of the teasing.

I'd called my mother from the dentist's office a few days after Jack's first visit to Maine. More cavities than expected, I told her. Would be late getting home.

"Better hurry. There's a long white florist box here for you. Came in the mail—from Bridgeport. Shall I open it?"

"Must be a thank-you from Jack, probably roses. But isn't he foolish to send them through the mail! They'll all be dead. Yes, open them—put them in water!"

Thrilled, I went back to the dentist's chair—gripped the arms and all through the drilling and filling comforted myself—*You can stand this, Clarine . . . Jack has sent you roses.*

He hadn't. Part of his visit had been spent at my brother's camp in the woods. Bugs had been vicious. Where black flies left off, mosquitoes took up. Inside the long white florist's box, wrapped in tissue paper, was a long metal bug sprayer, beside it a can of Flit.

The real roses came later. Only one at first—for my birthday, Christmas, our anniversary. When John was born, there were three—two deep red, one small white bud . . . for Lornagrace, second child, three red roses and again the tiny bud. So bouquets grew as the family grew until, in 1975, Jack sent to our daughter Pamela fourteen red roses and one white bud. A seventh grandchild had just been born.

Sometimes we had second-hand roses—great baskets of them left behind at weddings, funerals, christenings, carried home to the parsonage. Whether the source had been joy or sorrow, beginning or ending, roses were always welcome, their fragrant, fragile loveliness enjoyed.

Often we planted rose bushes, and so in time cut our own blossoms. Often previous pastors had done the same. In Darien, especially, we gloried in the long hedge of yellow, white, and pink roses lovingly nurtured by our predecessor, the Reverend Ken Greene. Summers in Maine we picked wild moss roses, growing along the coast, popping up unwanted in the blueberry barrens. Sometimes we harvested wild rose hips, big as tomatoes, crushed them and made pink, delicately flavored rose jelly.

Through the years, I often scolded my husband for his extravagance. "A rose corsage for Mother's Day? You just gave me one for Easter! What I really need is panty hose! And you need a haircut!" Scolding had no effect. Roses kept coming—even when we were old, even in Alaska. . . .

I can see Jack standing there in the airport at Anchorage—an old man now, white-haired, a bit stooped, waiting patiently for the

porter to push an old woman in a wheelchair through the barrier—old, yes, but in his eyes the same intense, expectant look of love, and in his arms still, after all those years, roses . . . a dozen deep red, long-stemmed, American Beauty roses. Do you have any idea how much roses cost in Alaska?

I had exactly one five-dollar bill in my purse when I left Hartford for the six-thousand-mile flight to Anchorage. Bill Carroll, friend and pastor, pushed my wheelchair through the door marked *Departures.*

"Bill, would you get this five changed to five ones?"

"Sure—want some magazines?" Bill had no idea of my financial condition. Six thousand miles on five dollars? I'd read the freebies in the elastic pocket.

"No, thanks—just need some change to tip the porters."

Bill brought the five ones, wished me Godspeed. The first porter pushed me down the ramp. At the door of the plane I gave him the first dollar bill. An hour later at O'Hare, I gave the second to the porter who pushed me from the plane to the waiting room. A two-hour layover. Did I dare buy coffee? a Danish? Better not. I gave the third dollar to the porter who pushed me back to the plane for the six-hour flight to Anchorage. I hoped they'd serve something besides pretzels.

They didn't—not much. Hungrier and hungrier as the hours passed . . . bored, the freebies all read, I asked myself how I'd gotten into this penniless predicament anyway. . . .

A summer in Alaska had seemed a marvelous idea in early June. Roger Thompson, long-time friend and fellow pastor, had invited Jack to fill his pulpit for July and August while the Thompsons attended a World Conference on Methodism in Ireland, traveled around a bit. It was 1976. Jack had been retired for three years, I for three months. He knew Anchorage, welcomed the chance to preach again. Swimming had increased my mobility. Often now I could do without the wheelchair. I could certainly do with a celebration, something special to mark the end of a teaching career spanning five decades.

Because of the teaching career, we could afford the trip. A fairly large one-time pension check would be coming July 1. So in June we put tickets for Alaska on the American Express card and put carpenters to work building a deck on our Maine camp. Surely they'd be finished by July 1.

They weren't. Jack flew to Anchorage alone to begin his interim pastorate. I stayed on to supervise carpenters and wait for the pension check to arrive. It didn't. In mid-July I called Hartford, the State Board of Education.

"Mrs. Grenfell? Your check? Oh, yes—that will be mailed out August 1."

"But I thought July—"

"No, no—August. That's the way the system works."

Who can argue with the way the system works? Jack had taken a fair amount of cash with him. I managed to pay the carpenters . . . drove to Hartford, boarded the plane with my five one-dollar bills, headed for Alaska. Jack would be waiting. He was bound to have money.

Have money! He certainly must! There he was now, standing with his arms full of roses! In a burst of gratitude and generosity, I double tipped the Anchorage porter, gave him the last two dollar bills.

"Darling," I cried as he filled my arms with roses, "I'm so glad to see you! What time is it here?"

"Three o'clock—"

"Well, could we go somewhere and have an early dinner? I'm really starved!"

He looked at me. "Did your pension check come, dear?"

"No—they'll mail it out the first of August."

"Well, I have a few dollars left. You've no idea how fast money goes in Alaska. The roses—"

So we drove through the familiar golden arches that are, thankfully, even in Alaska, and I feasted my eyes on my lapful of roses while I devoured two cheeseburgers.

The next morning I looked out the kitchen window and saw a large moose grazing on the Thompsons' lawn. I wished I'd packed Millard's old hunting rifle. Instead I stole a package of ground moose meat from the Thompsons' freezer. I also looked in the yellow pages, called the Anchorage Chapter of Overeaters Anonymous, joined up.

Parishioners, wondering if the distinguished pastor and his wife from the Lower Forty-eight were too busy to join them for a meal, were never disappointed—all invitations gladly, even ravenously, accepted. When the pension check finally arrived, we knew the parish rather well and I'd lost fourteen pounds.

So we replaced the stolen moose meat with ground beef and celebrated at last—went out to dinner, saw the parks and glaciers, even flew to Nome, inside the Arctic Circle.

Here on the shore one day—looking at long whaleboats, red slabs of salmon drying in the sun, sled dogs behind strong fences— I bent down and picked up a small, two-pronged piece of driftwood. Where had it come from? "You'll love Nome!" Servicemen assigned there in World War II used to be told. "There's a blonde behind every tree!" Yes, because there are, of course, no trees in Nome. Not one. Yet here was a piece of driftwood . . .

Two hundred miles across from the shore on which I stood was Russia. Had my bit of tree come from there, borne of the waves of the Bering Sea? Had Russian children once played in its shade? Russian sweethearts carved initials in its bark?

I would never know. I only know that driftwood in Nome is rare and precious—rare and precious as love that lasts across the years, rare and precious as memory . . .

Memory of a rare and gallant gentleman awaiting the arrival of an aged wife, pockets almost empty because he wants to welcome her with roses . . .

A rare and gallant gentleman who once invited a girl to come for a five-minute walk to see the roses . . . roses that never stopped blooming . . . a five-minute walk that lasted a lifetime . . . a walk that—who knows?—may one day be resumed.

Driftwood picked up in Nome where there are no trees, brought from the shore of the Bering Sea to the green park bench near the gazebo . . . driftwood, rare and precious. Where had it come from?

COMMUNICATION SKILLS

There is a way of speaking
With no word . . .
A way of conversing
With nothing heard . . .

There is a way of talking
Without sound . . .
The old way of telling
Lovers found . . .

An ancient telepathy
Known to the wise
Who send clear messages
From silent eyes . . . .

A rare and gallant gentleman,
Jack cuts a rose-decorated cake as
friends celebrated his 70th birth-
day with a gala Open House at
612 Fern Street, West Hartford,
Connecticut—home of the Gren-
fells for sixteen years.

133

INVOCATION

O Thou who art so far above and beyond us,
Yet upon whom we so completely depend,
Receive our gratitude for the air we breathe,
For the free-flowing waters of the world,
For the good earth that gives forth increase,
For plant and flower, bird and beast
That inhabit Thy great garden.

How wondrous Thou art!
Thou dost open Thine hand, and we are fed!

Yet we have despoiled the air,
We have made the waters unclean,
We have poisoned the earth until it turns sour.
Dost Thou forgive?

Help us, we pray, to sustain the sense of the sacred
In the stewardship of our living.
Grant us in this world, life
And, in the world to come, life everlasting. Amen.

The Reverend Jack Grenfell
Northeast Fish and Wildlife Conference
Hartford, Connecticut, January 19-22, 1964

THERE IS NO ONE THERE

Why are you driving so fast? There is no one there—
No one watching, waiting to call, "I'm glad you're home!"
The storm's so bad I've been worried about you, dear!"

Why are you driving so fast? Did you forget?
Did you think for a moment things are as they used to be—
Every window ablaze with light, the door flung wide,
Voices and laughter and love flowing out, "Mom's here . . .
Hi, Mom! Supper's ready . . . we've all been waiting for you!"

Why are you driving so fast? The house will be dark . . .
The mail still there in the box at the foot of the drive . . .
You'll fumble to fit the key, flick on the lights . . .
The stove will be cold, no kettle bubbling for tea . . .
Your coffee mug unwashed on the shelf by the sink . . .

Why are you driving so fast? There is no one there.
Slow down . . . slow down . . . There is no one waiting for you.

ABOUT THE AUTHOR . . .

Clarine Coffin Grenfell is a native of Bangor, Maine, but has spent much of her adult life as educator and writer in New York and Connecticut. She earned her Bachelor of Arts degree with Phi Beta Kappa honors at University of Maine and her Bachelor of Divinity at Hartford Theological Seminary. At various times she has been the pastor of Methodist churches, chairperson of departments of English, editor and reading consultant in the Educational Division of *Reader's Digest*. Married for many years to the late Reverend Jack Grenfell, she is the mother of a son and two daughters.

Following the publication of *The Caress and the Hurt* in 1982 and *Women My Husband Married* in 1983, *Roses in December* is the third in a series of autobiographical books written by Mrs. Grenfell. A popular speaker throughout her career, she especially enjoys traveling the country and sharing her 'prose and verse' with live audiences. Since 1982 these audiences have totaled more than twelve thousand people of all ages, plus an uncounted number via radio and television. If you would like to order books or to invite Mrs. Grenfell to come to your school, church, library, or club, you may write to Grenfell Reading Center, Orland, Maine 04472.